A Manual for the Wearing

of

Orders, Decorations and Medals

ANDREW HANHAM

SPINK

2005

69 Southampton Row, Bloomsbury
London WC1B 4ET
Telephone: 020 7563 4000
Fax: 020 7563 4066

ISBN 1-902040-60-0

Printed by Pardy & Son (Printers) Ltd
1 Parkside, Ringwood, Hampshire

Table of Contents

Acknowledgements   vi

Introduction   vii

1.   British Orders, Decorations and Medals   1

2.   Gazetting and Investitures   6

3.   Foreign and Commonwealth Orders, Decorations and Medals   12

4.   Occasions when Orders, Decorations and Medals are worn   17

5.   Order of Wear   21

6.   The Orders of Knighthood and other Insignia: general principles for wear   30

7.   Medals, Ribbons and Miniatures   35

8.   Gentlemen: Civilian Dress   51

9.   Ladies: Civilian Dress   62

10. The Armed Forces   72

11. Robes, Court Dress, Civil and Ceremonial Uniform   98

12. Services for the Orders of Knighthood   103

13. Miscellaneous matters   105

     (a) The return of insignia upon the decease of the holder
     (b) Loss and replacement of orders, decorations and medals
     (c) The wearing of medals by next-of-kin
     (d) Unofficial commemorative medals

14. Glossary of terms   108

Table 1:   Insignia requirements for Civilian Dress   110
Table 2:   Insignia requirements and restrictions for the Armed Forces   111

Appendix 1:   British campaign medals and clasps   112
Appendix 2:   UN, NATO and other international medals   115
Appendix 3:   Riband widths with insignia, and on ribbon bars   117
Appendix 4:   Permitted post-nominal letters for British Orders, Decorations
                 and Medals   119
Appendix 5:   Addresses   122

INDEX   124

Andrew Hanham is an historian, and is an expert on the British honours system and its history. He graduated at the University of Leicester in 1980, where he subsequently completed a doctoral thesis on British politics in the eighteenth century. He was for many years a senior member of the research staff of the History of Parliament Trust, and has taught at the Universities of Leicester and Cambridge. He is a Fellow of the Royal Historical Society.

Acknowledgements

The preparation of this work has benefited enormously from the assistance and expertise of many individuals and organisations, and I gratefully acknowledge the help given by Lieutenant Colonel Robert Cartwright, LVO, Secretary of the Central Chancery of the Orders of Knighthood; Mr. G. Attwater, MBE, the Royal Navy Stores Policy Officer; Lieutenant Commander Michael Lydon; Lieutenant Colonel Richard Bird, OBE, Major Robert Adams, Major Derek Burton, and Colonel Marion Lauder, MBE, of the Ministry of Defence; Major Nicholas Atkinson, of the Army Medals Office; Lieutenant Colonel Sally Cadec of the office of the Defence Services Secretary; Wing Commander John Davies, RAF Ceremonial Officer (rtd.); Sir Robert Balchin, Secretary of the Imperial Society of Knights Bachelor; Dr. Malcolm Golin; Mrs. Anne Johnson, MBE; Mr. William Hunt, TD, Windsor Herald of Arms, College of Arms; Dr. Clive Cheesman, Rouge Dragon Pursuivant of Arms, College of Arms; Mrs. Judith Jones, MBE, Clerk to the Lord Chief Justice; the Honours Secretariat of the Foreign and Commonwealth Office; Mr. John Hayward, Collectors Medals Department, Spink and Son Ltd.; Mr. Christopher Allan of Messrs. Ede and Ravenscroft; Messrs. Gieves and Hawkes; and Messrs. Watts and Company.

My sincerest thanks are due to Mr. Jeremy Bagwell Purefoy, MVO, Insignia Clerk at the Central Chancery of the Orders of Knighthood, who has given invaluable help and advice throughout the gestation of this work, and to Lieutenant Colonel Charles Webb for his exemplary skill and care with the illustrations. For editorial and administrative assistance I am grateful to Mr. David Guest, Mr. Oliver Pepys, Mr. Jonathan Arnold and Mr. Ian Copson of Spink & Son Ltd.

A.H.

Introduction

For as long as there have been royal or official 'marks of distinction' in recognition of achievement and service, there have been rules and regulations governing the way in which they were to be worn.

In the days before campaign and gallantry medals, the prestige and exclusiveness of an order of knighthood depended greatly upon its ensigns being worn correctly and consistently, and in a way that did honour to the wearer, to the order itself and to its sovereign. The statutes of particular orders usually prescribed the occasions on which insignia were to be worn and in what manner. In Britain, as in other European countries, the award of decorations and medals became a routine preoccupation of the military sphere from the early nineteenth century onwards. Initially, rules for wear were matters of regimental fashion, but from 1868 the Army's authorities began to lay down general requirements which did much to establish the accepted formats for the display of insignia and campaign medals, not only with army uniform but with most other types of official dress. An 'order of wear' began to evolve in the 1880s setting out the required sequence or precedence in which orders, decorations and medals were to be worn. The Lord Chamberlain's Office increased its authority over official dress, laying down regulations to be observed at Court and on all other social and ceremonial occasions. Details of dress requirements were routinely published in *The London Gazette* and included directions for the wearing of decorations with evening dress and the plethora of uniforms which up to the 1900s, and long afterwards, remained the official attire of ministers of state, ambassadors, proconsuls and a host of others. From time to time these Royal Household regulations were consolidated and published in a series of manuals, the last of which appeared in 1937 under the title, *Dress and Insignia worn at His Majesty's Court*. Since then, changing etiquette and the paring down of ceremonial have naturally tended to discourage the regular or even occasional updating of the available literature on the subject.

This Manual, while making no attempt to emulate the splendidly produced Court manuals of yesteryear, aims to fill the present need for a comprehensive new guide to the protocol and regulations for the wearing of orders, decorations and medals currently in force in the United Kingdom and its associated territories. It has been compiled with the assistance of the Central Chancery of the Orders of Knighthood, the Royal Household office within the Lord Chamberlain's Department which since 1904 has been responsible for all matters relating to the conferral and wearing of insignia. Close attention, too, has been paid to the most recent editions of the Dress Regulations for the three main branches of the Armed Forces, while other authorities and bodies have been consulted on matters relating to robes and other forms of ceremonial dress. A major objective has been to anticipate and explain particular issues on which uncertainty and confusion often arises. Sections 7 to 11 are accompanied by a series of illustrations which help to demonstrate the layout of medals and insignia with different styles of dress and uniform. To enhance 'user friendliness', a certain amount of repetition has been built into some Sections (particularly Sections 8 to 10), which has helped to retain overall clarity and minimise occasions on which the reader has to refer to other parts of the work.

SPINK

— FOUNDED 1666 —

Spink is housed in the old Post Office building in Bloomsbury near the British Museum. The interior of the five-storey Georgian building has been completely re-designed to our specifications, providing excellent auction and dealing facilities.

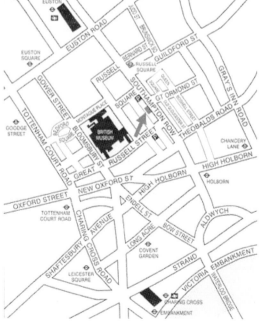

Office Hours:
Monday to Friday
9:30am to 5:30pm

Nearest Tube Stations:
Holburn or Russell Square

69 Southampton Row, Bloomsbury, London, WC1B 4ET
Telephone: +44 (0)20 7563 4000   Fax: +44 (0)20 7563 4066
Email: info@spink.com
www.spink.com

1. British Orders, Decorations and Medals

This section provides a brief summary of the honours and awards of the United Kingdom. While it is beyond the scope of this work to include a full photographic display of all the insignia concerned, what follows here is a brief guide to the Orders of Knighthood and other distinctions, arranged so that anyone who is largely unfamiliar with this territory will be able to identify the various honours, at least in terms of their basic appearance, and will enable them to determine, for instance, which insignia are worn as neck decorations as opposed to breast decorations which are worn in the same fashion as campaign medals. Where necessary, certain distinguishing features of some insignia have been highlighted in order to help clarify differences between items which are otherwise very similar in appearance.

● THE MOST NOBLE ORDER OF THE GARTER
Knight Companion and *Lady Companion* (KG and LG): wears the Breast Star on the left side, and a gold Badge (known as the 'Lesser George') attached to the Sash (or Broad Riband) which is worn over the left shoulder with the Badge resting on the right hip. The Collar, from which is suspended an enamel Badge (known as the 'George'), is worn on specified occasions. It is worn over the Order's Mantle at the annual services of the Order at St. George's Chapel, Windsor. Knights and Ladies Companion also receive as part of the Order's insignia a velvet 'garter' lettered in gold with the Order's motto.

● THE MOST ANCIENT AND MOST NOBLE ORDER OF THE THISTLE
Knight and *Lady* (KT and LT): wears the Breast Star on the left side, and a gold Badge attached to the Sash (or Broad Riband) which is worn over the left shoulder with the Badge resting on the right hip. The Collar, from which hangs the Badge Appendant, is worn on specified occasions. It is worn over the Order's Mantle at the services of the Order at St. Giles' Cathedral, Edinburgh.

● THE MOST HONOURABLE ORDER OF THE BATH (Military and Civil Divisions)
Note: In the three classes of the Order of the Bath the Military and Civil divisions are differentiated by the design of their respective stars and badges.

1. *Knight Grand Cross* and *Dame Grand Cross* (GCB), the First Class of the Order, wears the Breast Star of this class on the left side, and the Badge attached to the Sash (or Broad Riband) which is worn over the right shoulder with the Badge resting on the left hip. The Collar, which has its own Badge, is worn on specified occasions. Knights and Dames Grand Cross wear the Collar over the Order's Mantle at the services of the Order at Westminster Abbey and on other occasions by Royal command.

2. *Knight Commander* and *Dame Commander* (KCB and DCB), the Second Class of the Order, wears the Breast Star of this class on the left side, and the Badge, worn by

men (and women in uniform) as a neck decoration, and by women in civilian attire on a bow on the left side above the Star.

3. *Companion* (CB), the Third Class of the Order, wears the Badge; it is worn by men (and women in uniform) as a neck decoration, and by women in civilian attire on a bow on the left side.

* *The First and Second Classes of the Order bestow the titles of 'Sir' or 'Dame'.*

● THE MOST DISTINGUISHED ORDER OF ST. MICHAEL AND ST. GEORGE

1. *Knight Grand Cross* and *Dame Grand Cross* (GCMG), the First Class of the Order, wears the Breast Star of this class on the left side, and the Badge which ordinarily is attached to the Sash (or Broad Riband) which is worn over the right shoulder with the Badge resting on the left hip. On specified occasions the Badge is worn appended from the Order's Collar. Knights and Dames Grand Cross wear the Collar over the Order's Mantle at the services of the Order at St. Paul's Cathedral and on other occasions by Royal command.

2. *Knight Commander* and *Dame Commander* (KCMG and DCMG), the Second Class of the Order, wears the Breast Star of this class on the left side, and the Badge, worn by men (and women in uniform) as a neck decoration, and by women in civilian attire on a bow on the left side above the Star.

3. *Companion* (CMG), the Third Class of the Order, wears the Badge; it is worn by men (and women in uniform) as a neck decoration, and by women in civilian attire on a bow on the left side.

* *The First and Second Classes of the Order bestow the titles of 'Sir' or 'Dame'.*

● THE ROYAL VICTORIAN ORDER

1. *Knight Grand Cross* and *Dame Grand Cross* (GCVO), the First Class of the Order, wears the Breast Star of this class on the left side, and the Badge which ordinarily is attached to the Sash (or Broad Riband) which is worn over the right shoulder with the Badge resting on the left hip. On specified occasions the Badge is worn appended from the Order's Collar. Knights and Dames Grand Cross wear the Collar over the Order's Mantle at services of the Order held at St. George's Chapel, Windsor, and on other occasions by Royal command.

2. *Knight Commander* and *Dame Commander* (KCVO and DCVO), the Second Class of the Order, wears the Breast Star of this class on the left side, and the Badge, worn by men (and women in uniform) as a neck decoration, and by women in civilian attire on a bow on the left side above the Star.

3. *Commander* (CVO), the Third Class of the Order, wears the Badge; it is worn by men (and women in uniform) as a neck decoration, and by women in civilian attire on a bow on the left side.

4. *Lieutenant* (LVO), the Fourth Class of the Order, wears the Breast Badge (in enamel) on the left side; it is worn by men (and women in uniform) on a short chest riband, and on a bow by women in civilian attire.

5. *Member* (MVO), the Fifth Class of the Order, wears the Breast Badge (in frosted silver) on the left side; it is worn by men (and women in uniform) on a short chest riband, and on a bow by women in civilian attire.

   The Royal Victorian Medal (RVM), is the associate medal of the Royal Victorian Order, and is awarded in gold, silver and bronze. It is worn on the left side on a short chest riband by men (and women in uniform), and on a bow by women in civilian attire.

* The First and Second Classes of the Order bestow the titles of 'Sir' or 'Dame'.

● **THE MOST EXCELLENT ORDER OF THE BRITISH EMPIRE** (Military and Civil Divisions)
Note: In the five classes of the Order of the British Empire appointment to the Military Division is distinguished from the Civil Division by a narrow central stripe of pearl grey on the Order's rose-pink riband.

1. *Knight Grand Cross* and *Dame Grand Cross* (GBE), the First Class of the Order, wears the Breast Star of this class on the left side, and the Badge which ordinarily is attached to the Sash (or Broad Riband) which is worn over the right shoulder with the Badge resting on the left hip. On specified occasions the Badge is worn appended from the Order's Collar. Knights and Dames Grand Cross wear the Collar over the Order's Mantle at the services of the Order at St. Paul's Cathedral and on other occasions by Royal command.

2. *Knight Commander* and *Dame Commander* (KBE or DBE), the Second Class of the Order, wears the Breast Star of this class on the left side, and the Badge, worn by men (and women in uniform) as a neck decoration, and by women in civilian attire on a bow on the left side above the Star.

3. *Commander* (CBE), the Third Class of the Order, wears the Badge; it is worn by men (and women in uniform) as a neck decoration, and by women in civilian attire on a bow on the left side.

4. *Officer* (OBE), the Fourth Class of the Order, wears the Breast Badge (in silver-gilt) on the left side; it is worn by men (and women in uniform) on a short chest riband, and on a bow by women in civilian attire.

5. *Member* (MBE), the Fifth Class of the Order, wears the Breast Badge (in silver) on the left side; it is worn by men (and women in uniform) on a short chest riband, and on a bow by women in civilian attire.

   The British Empire Medal (BEM), is the associate medal of the Order, but ceased to be awarded in the United Kingdom in 1993. It continues to be awarded in several Commonwealth countries. The silver medal is worn on the left side, on a short chest riband by men (and women in uniform), and on a bow by women in civilian attire.

* The First and Second Classes of the Order bestow the titles of 'Sir' or 'Dame'.

● The **ORDER OF MERIT** (OM), and the **ORDER OF THE COMPANIONS OF HONOUR** (CH) are single-class distinctions, neither of which bestows any rank or title. The badges of these Orders are worn as neck decorations by men, and by women as bow decorations on the left side. The Order of Merit has a Civil and a Military Division, although the latter has not been awarded since 1965.

● The **Royal Victorian Chain** is quite distinct from, and has no connection with, the Royal Victorian Order, despite the fact that its Badge is identical. The badge is suspended from a shortened chain and is worn around the neck. When worn by women it is in the form of a bow and tails mounting of the riband of the Royal Victorian Order, to which four links of the Chain are attached, and from which the Badge is suspended; it is worn on the left side. An award of the Chain bestows no rank or title.

● The oval Badge of a **Baronet** is a neck decoration worn by men. There are two main types of Baronets' Badge, each with its own riband, one of which denotes a Baronet created of Nova Scotia, the other a Baronet created of England, Ireland, Great Britain or of the United Kingdom. The latter Badge uses different motifs within its design to signify the category in which a baronetcy was created.

● The insignia of a **Knight Bachelor** consists of a Badge worn as a neck decoration, and a pin-backed Breast Badge or 'star'.

All other principal honours and awards are breast decorations, badges or medals suspended from short chest ribands (or from bows if worn singly by ladies who are not uniformed personnel), and worn on the left side:

● Two other 'Orders', the **Distinguished Service Order** (DSO) and the **Imperial Service Order** (ISO), are single-class awards. The latter has not been awarded in the UK since 1993 but is still awarded in certain Commonwealth countries.

● The **Victoria Cross** (VC) and the **George Cross** (GC) head the list of breast decorations for gallantry and take precedence over all other awards. They are followed by the **Conspicuous Gallantry Cross** (CGC), the **Distinguished Service Cross** (DSC), the **Military Cross** (MC), and the **Distinguished Flying Cross** (DFC).

● The **Royal Red Cross** is awarded in two classes, the First Class Badge (RRC) in gold, and the Second Class Badge of 'Associate' (ARRC) in frosted silver.

● From this point on, most modern awards conform to the standard appearance of medals, being of circular form and usually in silver. These are broadly classifiable as: gallantry medals, campaign medals, long/meritorious service medals, and commemorative medals (coronation, jubilee, etc.). Those which are currently awarded (and many that are no longer awarded) are listed in Section 5, 'Order of Wear'.

● A further group of awards are in the form of emblems which are worn either on medal ribands (or ribbons), or directly on the uniform or coat. These emblems denote: **Mention(s) in Despatches**; the **Queen's Commendation for Bravery**; the **Queen's Commendation for Bravery in the Air**; and the **Queen's Commendation for Valuable Service**.

● THE MOST VENERABLE ORDER OF THE HOSPITAL OF ST. JOHN OF JERUSALEM
The Order of St. John enjoys the patronage of The Queen who is the Sovereign Head of the Order, but it does not form part of the honours of the Crown. Awards of the Order are made by its governing body, the Grand Priory of the Order, and not on the recommendation of HM Government. None of the Grades of the Order bestows any rank or title, and postnominal letters are not officially used to denote membership. The Order nevertheless has its place in the 'order of wear' and its insignia are worn by recipients with other orders, decorations and medals. The insignia of each Grade of the Order is as follows:

1. *Bailiff Grand Cross* and *Dame Grand Cross*, wears the Breast Star of this grade, viz. in gold without lion and unicorn embellishments, on the left side, and the Badge (enamel in gold setting) attached to the Sash (or Broad Riband) worn over the right shoulder with the Badge resting on the left hip. A smaller version of the Badge may be worn from a neck riband by men, or by women in civilian dress from a bow on the left side. The Order has no collar or chain.

2. *Knight of Justice* and *Dame of Justice*, wears the Breast Star of this grade, viz. in gold without lion and unicorn embellishments, on the left side, and the Badge (enamel in gold setting), worn by men (and women in uniform) from a neck riband, or by women in civilian dress on a bow on the left side above the Star.

3. *Knight of Grace* and *Dame of Grace*, wears the Breast Star of this grade, viz. in silver with lion and unicorn embellishments, on the left side, and the Badge (enamel in silver setting), worn by men (and women in uniform) from a neck riband, or by women in civilian dress on a bow on the left side above the Star.

4. *Commander (Brother/Sister)*, wears the Badge (enamel in silver setting); it is worn from a neck riband by men (and women in uniform), or on a bow on the left side by women in civilian dress.

5. *Officer (Brother/Sister)*, wears the Badge (enamel in silver setting) on the left side; it is worn by men (and women in uniform) on a short chest riband, or by women in civilian dress on a bow.

6. *Serving Brother* and *Serving Sister*, wears the Badge (in silver) on the left side; it is worn by men (and women in uniform) on a short chest riband, or from a bow by women in civilian dress.

Note: the Order of St. John is not administered by the Central Chancery of the Orders of Knighthood, and inquiries regarding the Order should be directed to its Chancery at the address given in Appendix 5.

2. Gazetting and Investitures

Gazetting of honours and awards

● *Gazettes and announcements*
The names of those who have been awarded honours are officially announced in *The London Gazette*. Two main lists are published each year: the 'New Year Honours', published on 31 December (or 30 December if New Year's Day is a Monday), and the 'Queen's Birthday Honours' published on the second or third Saturday in June. These lists are usually also published in the major newspapers.

At other times during the year *The London Gazette* publishes smaller lists which are more specialist in focus. There are usually two lists each year in relation to operations by the Armed Forces, and two for acts of gallantry by Police and Fire Services personnel, and by civilians. Promotions in, or appointments to, the Order of St. John are published in separate lists in the *Gazette*. There are also separate lists in respect of the Polar Medal, and the Imperial Service Medal. Announcements of honours are made upon the dissolution of a Parliament, upon the resignation of a government, and to mark special Royal events, such as a coronation, jubilee, or birthday, or following the demise of a senior Member of the Royal Family.

There are periodic announcements, also published in the *Gazette*, of individual awards, such as knighthoods and DBEs to high court judges.

Appointments to honours in the exclusive personal gift of The Queen, namely the Order of the Garter, the Order of the Thistle, and the Order of Merit, are also separately announced, as are occasional appointments to the Royal Victorian Order that are additional to those included in the two main Honours Lists.

Honorary awards to non-British citizens who have made important contributions to British interests at home or abroad are very rarely gazetted, but may be announced by means of a press release from the Foreign and Commonwealth Office.

● *Use of titles and post-nominal letters (Knights and Dames)*
Individuals who are promoted to, or appointed to the class of Knight or Dame Grand Cross, or Knight or Dame Commander in one of the Orders of Knighthood, may (if they are not already peers, peeresses, baronets or knights) assume the prefix title of "Sir" or "Dame" with immediate effect from the date of the official announcement in the *Gazette*. They may also with immediate effect use the post-nominal letters denoting the honour where it is appropriate to do so, eg. "Sir --- ---, KCVO" and "Dame --- ---, DBE".

Similarly, gentlemen who are appointed Knight Bachelor may use the prefix title of "Sir" with immediate effect of the announcement, but do not use post-nominal letters to denote their rank of Knight Bachelor.

Clergymen who are appointed Knight Grand Cross or Knight Commander in an Order of Knighthood do not use the prefix title of "Sir" and do not receive the accolade of knighthood. With immediate effect from the announcement of the award he may use the appropriate post-nominal letters, eg. "The Very Rev. Dr --- ---, KCVO".

The wives of Knights Grand Cross, Knights Commander or Knights Bachelor may, with immediate effect of the announcement of their husbands' award, assume the title of "Lady", but use only their surname, not their Christian name, in the title, eg. "Lady Macbeth". The wives of Clergymen do not use the title of "Lady".

● *Use of post-nominal letters (other awards)*
The recipients of many other honours are entitled, with immediate effect of the announcement, to use the appropriate post-nominal letters, eg. "--- --- Esq., CBE", "Wing Commander, --- ---, DFC", or "Chief Constable --- ---, QPM". A list of honours currently awarded whose statutes allow the use of post-nominal letters can be found at Appendix 4.

● *Wearing of Miniatures*
The recipient of an award may, with immediate effect of the announcement, wear the appropriate miniature badge, decoration or medal, even though there will be a lapse of time before the award itself is actually presented.

● *Commencement of wear ribbon*
Members of the Armed Forces, and other personnel in uniform, should with immediate effect of the announcement, wear the ribbon of the award. When situated with other ribbons it should be worn in its correct place in the 'order of wear'.

● *Honorary awards*
The recipients of honorary knighthoods receive the insignia of a Knight Grand Cross or of Knight Commander in one of the Orders of Knighthood. They may not use the prefix title of "Sir" (or their wives the title of "Lady"), but can use the appropriate post-nominal letters after their name, eg. "Mr. --- ---, KBE". Similarly, ladies who become honorary Dames Grand Cross or Dame Commanders may not use the title of "Dame", but are entitled to use the post-nominal letters of the award, eg. "Mrs. --- ---, DBE". Should the recipient subsequently become a British subject then his/her honourary award becomes a full one, and the style of 'Sir' or 'Dame' may be adopted. The post-nominal letters of less senior awards may be used in the same fashion, eg. "Mr. --- ---, OBE". In these circumstances, gentlemen will be required to attend an investiture in order to receive the accolade of knighthood.

● *Armorial Bearings*
Persons who are armigerous and who become members of any class of the Orders of Knighthood, or become Knights Bachelor, members of any grade of the Order of St. John, or who are awarded a decoration or medal for gallantry, are entitled to represent their insignia with their armorial bearings. Anyone who does not have arms may, if they wish, petition for a grant of arms after receiving an honour, and the insignia will

be represented with the arms in the manner laid down in the Statutes of the honour concerned. Those who are considering either course are advised to consult the Officer-in-Waiting at the College of Arms. Recipients who are of Scottish birth, or resident in Scotland, should contact the Court of Lord Lyon in Edinburgh. (The full addresses may be found in Appendix 5).

Investitures

Investitures are held at Buckingham Palace where awards are presented by The Queen or another Member of the Royal Family on her behalf. There are usually about twenty investitures a year at the Palace with an additional one at the Palace of Holyroodhouse in Edinburgh, and another in Cardiff. Around 100 individuals receive their awards at each investiture, and recipients may be accompanied by up to three guests. Investitures may sometimes be held overseas by The Queen on a State Visit, or on a visit by a Member of the Royal Family.

Those who are appointed Knights of the Garter, and of the Thistle, and Members of the Orders of Merit, and of the Companions of Honour are received privately in audience and presented with their insignia. The Queen also receives and invests privately some recipients of the Royal Victorian Order who have rendered personal service to herself or the Royal Family.

● *Awards given at Investiture*
The Central Chancery of the Orders of Knighthood at St. James's Palace will summon recipients to Buckingham Palace for investiture if they are to receive the following awards: the Victoria Cross, the George Cross, the insignia of one of the Orders of Knighthood, the accolade of Knighthood, the Distinguished Service Order, the Royal Red Cross, a decoration or medal awarded for gallantry or (in some cases) meritorious service, the Polar Medal, or the Royal Victorian Medal.

● *Residence abroad*
Those who are serving or resident abroad, and who are unable to attend an investiture in the United Kingdom, or who are unlikely to be in the United Kingdom for some considerable time, may elect to have their award presented by a representative of The Queen, who will usually be an Ambassador, High Commissioner or Governor-General.

● *Ill-health or temporary service abroad*
If a person is unable to attend an investiture due to ill-health, or service abroad, their attendance may be deferred to a more convenient time. In cases where attendance is prevented by permanent ill-health, arrangements can be made for the insignia to be presented by a local representative of The Queen, such as the Lord-Lieutenant of a county, or it can be sent by post.

● *Presentations of commendation awards, long service medals, etc.*
Uniformed personnel who are mentioned in despatches, commended for bravery, bravery in the air or for valuable service, or who are awarded medals for meritorious service or for long service and good conduct, will receive their awards at a parade or ceremony arranged by the commanding officer. Civilians who are to receive commendations will be presented with their awards by a local representative of The Queen, or a Government Minister.

● *Posthumous awards*
When posthumous awards for gallantry are made, the family of the deceased (up to four) will be received privately and the award will be presented before a main investiture. Where a person has died after his or her award was announced, the next-of-kin (the widow, son, daughter, etc.) will attend a main investiture and be presented with the insignia on the recipient's behalf.

● *Dress requirements at investitures*
Members of the armed and public services wear uniform at investitures, but may not wear the insignia of any other orders, decorations and medals; medal ribbons only are to be worn with uniform, including that for the award which is to be received. Retired officers of the Armed Forces may wear uniform. Otherwise, gentlemen may wear morning dress or dark lounge suit, and ladies should wear day dress, preferably with a hat.

Immediately after an investiture, recipients of awards are given a case for containing the insignia, together with brief instructions for wearing them. Warrants of Appointment are forwarded from the Central Chancery.

Order of St. John of Jerusalem. Investitures of the Bailiffs and Dames Grand Cross, and of Knights and Dames of the Order are held at St. James's Palace approximately once every three years, and are conducted by the Grand Prior or his representative. Due to the lapse of time between each investiture, those newly gazetted may wear their insignia with immediate effect. In respect of the lower grades of the Order (namely Commander, Officer and Serving Brother or Sister), investitures are held four times a year at the Priory Church of St. John, Clerkenwell, and are conducted by the Prior of England and the Islands. Arrangements for the investitures are made by the Order's Headquarters.

Promotion in the Orders of Knighthood

● *Accolade of Knighthood*
Those who are appointed to knighthoods in one of the Orders of Knighthood, or who are appointed Knight Bachelor, receive at an investiture (or private audience) the 'accolade of knighthood', the tapping of each shoulder with a sword by The Queen. However, the accolade is not conferred again if subsequently a Knight Bachelor becomes a Knight Commander, or if a Knight Commander is promoted in the same

Order or is given the First or Second Class of another Order. On these occasions the recipient is simply invested with the insignia of the further award. Alternatively, a peer who is appointed to a knighthood in one of the Orders will also receive the accolade if it has not previously been conferred on him, even though he will not be using the prefix title of "Sir" to which the knighthood would otherwise entitle him. Foreign citizens awarded honorary knighthoods receive only the insignia of their awards and do not have the accolade conferred on them.

● *Return of insignia*
When a member of one of the Orders of Knighthood is promoted to a higher class in the same Order (and within the *same division* in the Orders of the Bath, and of the British Empire), the insignia of the lower grade may continue to be worn until the new insignia is received. From the date of the announcement of the award the postnominal letters only of the higher class should be used. Individuals will at some point be asked to return the insignia they hold of the lower class to the Central Chancery of the Orders of Knighthood. These requirements do not, of course, affect any awards in the other Orders of Knighthood which an individual may also hold. (Arrangements for the return of insignia upon the decease of the holder are explained in Section 13)

Although not an Order of Knighthood, the Decoration of Royal Red Cross (Second Class) should be returned to the Secretary of State for Defence if the holder is advanced to the First Class.

Insignia of the Order of St. John are not returnable on promotion within the Order.

'Double awards' in the Orders of Knighthood

There are a few exceptions to the general rule concerning the return of insignia upon promotion which allow certain awards in an Order of Knighthood to be held concurrently.

● *The Royal Victorian Order and the Royal Victorian Medal*
The Royal Victorian Medal (awarded in gold, silver or bronze) is the associate medal of the Royal Victorian Order. Any person who receives this medal in more than one category may wear them both together on the medal-bar. Subsequent awards of the same grade are denoted by the addition of a bar attached to the riband (men), or to the centre of the bow (ladies). The medal is retained and worn with the insignia of any class of the Royal Victorian Order which a medal-holder may subsequently receive. The recipient also continues to use the post-nominal letters 'RVM'.

● *The Orders of the Bath, and of the British Empire: Military and Civil Divisions.*
In the Orders of the Bath, and of the British Empire, both of which have Military and Civil Divisions, a person who holds the lower class of one division and who is promoted to a higher class in the other division, is permitted to retain and wear, additionally, the insignia of the lower class. This situation is unlikely to occur nowadays with the Order of the Bath but does arise with awards to the Order of the

British Empire. Accordingly, the holder of an MBE in the Military Division, on being advanced to OBE or CBE (or higher) in the same Division, would be required to return the junior insignia, but would retain it if advanced to OBE or CBE in the Civil Division. The post-nominal letters of the higher award only may be used.

● *The Order of the British Empire: the British Empire Medal*
The British Empire Medal is the associate medal of the Order of the British Empire. It ceased to be awarded to UK subjects in 1993, but continues in use in several Commonwealth countries. The medal consists of a single class but awards to military personnel are distinguished from those to civilians by a narrow grey central stripe on the riband. Subsequent awards are denoted by a bar attached to the riband (men), or to the centre of the bow (ladies). The medal is distinct from the Order, and is retained if the recipient is appointed to any class of the Order. The recipient also continues to use the post-nominal letters 'BEM'.

● *The Order of the British Empire: Gallantry awards*
A separate category of awards in the Order of the British Empire was made between 1957 and 1974 for acts of gallantry. Such awards were most usually in the form of the OBE, MBE or BEM, and were of either the Military or Civil Division, with the riband bearing a silver emblem of two crossed oakleaves. These awards in the Order are held independently and irrespective of any non-gallantry award(s) in the Order; it was also permissible for gallantry recipients on receiving a promotion, also for gallantry, to retain and wear the earlier insignia received. Thus a person awarded an OBE (Civil) for Gallantry between 1957 and 1974 might receive and wear with it the insignia of any class of the Order including that of a non-gallantry OBE (Civil). Holders of two or more awards in the Order, whether for gallantry or otherwise, are permitted to use only the post-nominal letters for the higher award. Gallantry awards in the Order ceased in 1974 and were superseded by the institution of the Queen's Gallantry Medal (QGM).

● *Knight Bachelor*
A Knight Bachelor who is subsequently appointed to a knighthood in one of the Orders of Knighthood, retains and may continue to wear his Knight Bachelor's insignia. Knight Bachelors who are subsequently advanced to the peerage may also continue to wear their insignia. Post-nominal letters are not used, however, to denote the rank of Knight Bachelor.

3. Foreign and Commonwealth Orders, Decorations and Medals

General

Foreign awards are those made by (i) the governments of foreign nations; (ii) Commonwealth nations of which The Queen is not the Sovereign; and (iii) international organisations such as the United Nations or NATO. A foreign order, decoration or medal may not be accepted and worn by British subjects unless prior permission to do so has been granted by The Queen. A recommendation for an award in civilian circumstances is usually made by a foreign government through its embassy in London to the Foreign and Commonwealth Office.

In the case of awards for military service, nominations or requests to receive and wear a foreign decoration will be passed through the chain of command to the Defence Services Secretary who will refer the matter to the Foreign and Commonwealth Office.

All recommendations for foreign awards require the agreement of the FCO and the Ceremonial Secretariat of the Cabinet Office before The Queen's permission is sought. If granted, approval of the award will be subject either to 'unrestricted', or to 'restricted' permission for the insignia to be worn by the recipient.

It may sometimes happen that foreign medals are presented to service personnel abroad without prior notice or warning. In such circumstances, a grateful acceptance should be the proper response. Notification of the award should then be submitted to the chain of command accompanied by a request for permission to wear it. Should such permission not be forthcoming, the recipient will usually be allowed to retain the medal as a keepsake.

(a) Unrestricted Permission
If 'unrestricted permission' is granted for a particular foreign order, decoration or medal to be worn, the recipient is entitled to wear the insignia or medal on all occasions when British insignia are worn, without any restriction. The Foreign and Commonwealth Office (or the Ministry of Defence, if the award is for military services) makes the necessary arrangement for a Warrant of approval to be prepared and signed by The Queen and for a notice to be published in *The London Gazette* announcing that such permission has been granted to the individual concerned. The *Gazette* notice may take the form of an announcement relating to a single individual, or may cover a series of awards to military personnel as part of an operational Honours List.

Unrestricted permission may also be granted in respect of particular medals given by foreign governments or international bodies. This will apply mainly to campaign or commemorative medals where The Queen's permission for unrestricted wear of a particular medal is promulgated in a Defence Council Instruction issued by the

Ministry of Defence.   An announcement may also be made in the *Gazette*.   Thus where a medal has been granted to all participants in a particular theatre of war, or celebratory event, the grant of 'unrestricted permission' in respect of that medal entitles each recipient to wear it in precedence after their British medals at all times.

(b) Restricted Permission

If 'restricted' permission is granted for wearing a foreign order, decoration or medal, the recipient receives notification to this effect from the Private Secretary to The Queen together with instructions that the insignia may be worn on specific occasions which will include any or all of the following:

(i)   In the presence of the Sovereign, Prince or Head of State of the nation or state to which the order, decoration or medal belongs.

(ii) In the presence of any other member of the Royal Family of the country concerned.

(iii) At the residence of any ambassador, minister or consular officer of that country, either in the United Kingdom or overseas.

(iv) When attached to, or when meeting officially any officers of the army, navy or air force, or any official deputation of the country concerned.

(v) At any official or semi-official ceremony held exclusively in connection with that country, such as a memorial service, the unveiling of a monument or the opening of an official institution.

(vi) On all official occasions while in that country.

In all other circumstances, foreign awards which have been accorded restricted permission only, may not be worn.

Commonwealth orders, decorations and medals

Awards from Commonwealth countries fall into two different categories depending on the constitutional status of individual member states:

(i) *Commonwealth countries of which The Sovereign is Head of State.* Some of these countries continue to bestow British honours, while others, as for example Australia, New Zealand, Canada and Jamaica, award honours which they themselves have instituted in the Sovereign's name.   Thus when any of the latter awards is gazetted to a British subject, the proposal will have been cleared in advance between the Commonwealth government making the award and the British government, and unrestricted permission to wear the insignia is granted.   Orders, decorations and medals of this category take precedence *after* all British honours.

(ii) *Commonwealth countries of which The Sovereign is not Head of State.* Permission to accept honours from Commonwealth countries which are republics, or indigenous monarchies such as the States of Malaysia and the State of Brunei, must be sought beforehand from The Sovereign.   If granted, permission will be subject, as with foreign awards, to either an 'unrestricted' or 'restricted' ruling. Orders, decorations and medals of this category take precedence *after* the honours of those Commonwealth countries in (i) above.

Protocol for wearing Foreign and Commonwealth orders, decorations and medals

● *'General' occasions.*
In the United Kingdom, on 'general' occasions, i.e. those not connected with a particular foreign or Commonwealth country, persons with 'unrestricted' permission to wear non-British awards should wear them *after* their British orders, decorations and medals. Persons with 'restricted' permission to wear insignia *do not* wear them on these occasions.

Foreign and Commonwealth insignia are arranged and worn according to the sequence laid down in the 'order of wear'. Senior insignia (breast stars, neck-badges) are, of course, subject to the numerical limitations for uniform or civilian dress; the decision as to which should be worn will be determined by seniority *or* date of award. If, for example, a person has the First Classes of two foreign orders, and wishes to wear only one of the breast stars, the earlier of the two awarded will be worn. If a person has the First Class of one order, awarded *after* the Second Class of another, the star of the former, being the senior, will be worn.

Some individuals may possess a higher class of a foreign award (for which they have unrestricted permission) than they have of a British order. In such circumstances the British award or awards will still take precedence. At a full evening dress function, for example, a person who holds the First Class of a foreign order and the Second Class of a British order, will wear the broad riband and badge of the foreign order and its breast star, but will wear the Second Class star of the British order in a position *senior* to that of the foreign First Class star (plus, of course, the associate neck-badge of the British order). If, however, the minister, ambassador or other representative of the country from which a person has an award is also a guest at a 'general' occasion, the foreign star should take precedence over the British star.

With regard to insignia worn on the medal-bar (full-size and miniature), the 'order of wear' specifies that these must be arranged with the orders of each country first, followed by the decorations of each country next, and the medals of each country last. Where there are awards from two or more countries, it is incorrect to have *all three* categories of insignia (i.e. orders, decorations and medals) grouped together for each country, followed by a similar grouping for another country.

If there are orders (or decorations, or medals) from several countries, the country order in which they are arranged is determined by date of award, with the earliest first. If there are two or more orders of the same country, the date of the senior award (according to the rules of precedence established in that country) dictates the place of that country's orders in the overall sequence. The same principles apply in the arrangement of decorations and medals (see p. 44).

- *'Specific' occasions.*

On any of the occasions listed above p.13, from (i) to (vi), the insignia of the country concerned, whether foreign or Commonwealth, should be worn in 'pride of place' *before* all British orders, decorations and medals. This applies equally to persons who have both unrestricted and restricted permission to wear the insignia. It is of course essential that foreign insignia are worn in a manner that ensures that due honour and regard are paid to a particular country when and where circumstances require.

The observance of this principle means that in practice a foreign First Class broad riband and badge should always be worn in preference to a British one; a foreign breast star, even if of the Second, rather than the First Class of an order, should always be worn in a position senior to that of any British First Class star; and a foreign neck-badge should always be worn in a senior position to, or instead of, a British one. If a person does not have the First Class of an order of the country concerned, he or she may wear instead the First Class broad riband and badge of a British order if it has been bestowed.

Persons who have 'restricted' permission to wear the suspended breast badge of an order or a decoration or medal, and who attend an event relating to the donor country, should wear the item in line with, and *in front* of, any British decorations and medals worn singly, or mounted in a group. The award should be separately attached to the coat or uniform using its individual brooch-pin. If the event is an evening occasion a miniature of the award is worn *in front* of miniatures of British awards. An order, decoration or medal which, on the other hand, has been accorded 'unrestricted' permission, enabling it to be worn on all occasions, will, in most cases, be included on a mounted group and sewn into place after British awards. However, when attending an event relating to the donor country it is *not* expected that the award be detached from its usual position in order to be worn in first place. The same applies to miniatures.

At a function in honour of a particular nation, it is permissible for the insignia of other foreign and Commonwealth countries to be worn, provided unrestricted permission to wear them has been granted. Such insignia must, however, be worn in accordance with the usual rules of precedence *after* all British insignia. Insignia of other countries accorded 'restricted' permission may *not* be worn.

As a general rule, British officers serving in a foreign country from whose Sovereign or Head of State they have received an award (which has been accorded either unrestricted or restricted permission), should wear the appropriate insignia whenever the officers of that country wear theirs.

Additional points

- *Stars and badges.* When the regulations of a foreign order or decoration require breast stars and/or badges to be worn on the *right* side of the breast, such regulations must be observed when these insignia are worn by British nationals with uniform or civilian clothes.

● *Mounted orders, decorations and medals (full-size and miniature).* As stated above, foreign or Commonwealth decorations and medals which have 'unrestricted' permission may be permanently incorporated *after* British medals on full-size and miniature brooch-bars. Before this is done, however, the recipient would be well-advised to consider whether he or she is likely to be attending events or functions on a regular basis where it would be more appropriate for the decoration or medal to take precedence over British awards. If this is the case, the decoration or medal should be kept unmounted in order that it may be worn when necessary in front of British awards. Members of the Armed Forces, diplomatic staff, and others engaged in periods of prolonged service in a foreign country, may choose to have any decorations or medals of that country mounted *in front* of their British awards. It may be included on a brooch-bar *after* British awards at a later date when an individual's regular association with a particular country has ceased. Persons with only 'restricted' permission to wear a decoration or medal of a particular country should not have it mounted with any British awards unless they are serving continuously over a prolonged period of time within the donor country.

● *Ribbons.* The ribbons of orders, decorations and medals which have been accorded unrestricted permission are worn on all occasions with other ribbons on undress uniform. Whether they should be incorporated *before* or *after* those for British awards will depend on the circumstances outlined in the preceding paragraph. Ribbons in respect of awards for which a person has received only restricted permission should not be worn, unless he or she is stationed in the donor country for an extended period of time. If the latter is the case, they should take precedence *before* the ribbons of British awards, and be removed when the period of service ends.

4. Occasions when Orders, Decorations and Medals are worn

When there is a requirement for orders, decorations and medals to be worn at a particular event or function, the manner in which they are worn is to a large extent determined by the type of occasion it is and the degree of formality to be observed. Broadly speaking, the occasions on which decorations are worn fall into two main categories: daytime occasions of a ceremonial or formal nature; and evening functions.

Daytime Occasions and Functions

It is impossible to provide a definitive list of the kinds of daytime occasions when medals are worn, or should be worn. Such events vary considerably in scale from major state ceremonial occasions involving The Queen and other Members of the Royal Family, down to occasions of a local nature where, possibly, only one or two dignitaries, such as the Lord-Lieutenant of a county, will be wearing medals.

The appropriate authority or officer responsible for organising an event should state if there is a requirement for medals to be worn. If an event is to be attended by The Queen or a Member, or Members of the Royal Family, and there is any uncertainty as to the question of wearing medals, the appropriate Royal Household should be consulted. If an event is of a religious nature, the ecclesiastical authority for the church or cathedral involved, or other convening authority, should likewise be consulted. In respect of events involving members of the Armed Forces, whether Single or Joint Service occasions, directions will be issued by the officer in command. There are also numerous situations where members of the Armed Forces personnel, individually or severally, will be required to wear medals on occasions of duty or minor ceremonial.

In the course of their duties, members of the Armed Forces follow a dress code (on which medal-wearing requirements are based) which classifies occasions as 'full ceremonial', 'ceremonial' and 'non-ceremonial', depending on the type and scale of event. 'Full ceremonial' occasions are usually those attended by The Queen and/or other Members of the Royal Family, and have a state or national significance, or which otherwise have a special importance to the Armed Forces, such as ceremonial inspections by a Commander-in-Chief. Ceremonial occasions are those where the degree of formality is less apparent but which nevertheless are important enough in themselves to warrant the wearing of insignia and medals. Non-ceremonial occasions are those which are low-key and strictly informal and where medal ribbons only are worn with uniform.

The occasions listed below are those on which orders, decorations and medals are usually worn:-

● Major ceremonial occasions at which the Sovereign is present (e.g. the State Opening of Parliament: ceremonial participants, peers, peeresses, guest ambassadors, etc.)

● The Sovereign's Birthday Parade (Trooping the Colour): the Sovereign's party and parade personnel (spectators who are members of services wear uniform and medal ribbons only).

● State visits by foreign Monarchs and Heads of State: those in attendance, and guards of honour.

● Special religious services of thanksgiving or memorial services, especially those attended by the Sovereign and/or Members of the Royal Family.

● Services of the Orders of Knighthood, and of the Order of St. John of Jerusalem.

● Parades and reviews of the Armed Forces, tattoos, inspections, and similar occasions at which the Sovereign and/or Members of the Royal Family is present (officer taking salute, official party and parade personnel – as directed).

● Parades to confer Freedoms of cities; to present a Queen's Colour, Squadron Standard or Personal Banner; Joint Service parades; Passing out parades.

● Festivals of Remembrance at the Royal Albert Hall; Remembrance Day parades; Battle of Britain parades and ex-Servicemen's gatherings.

● Military funerals and memorial services, i.e. of high-ranking officers and those who have rendered exceptional services to the nation: pall bearers and those attending in official or representative capacity.

● Escorts to senior Members of the Royal Family.

● Guards on duty in London and Edinburgh; garrison duty (as ordered by the district commander).

● Guards at Royal residences.

● Other occasions as specifically ordered.

Evening Functions

Orders, decorations and medals are worn with civilian evening dress or mess dress on the occasions listed below in accordance with instructions which have been published by the Lord Chamberlain's Office in *The London Gazette*:

(a) At parties, dinners and other functions when any of the following members of the Royal Family are present:

Her Majesty The Queen
His Royal Highness the Duke of Edinburgh
Their Royal Highnesses the Prince of Wales and Duchess of Cornwall
His Royal Highness the Duke of York
Their Royal Highnesses the Earl and Countess of Wessex
Her Royal Highness the Princess Royal
Their Royal Highnesses the Duke and Duchess of Gloucester
Their Royal Highnesses the Duke and Duchess of Kent
Their Royal Highnesses Prince and Princess Michael of Kent
Her Royal Highness Princess Alexandra, the Hon. Lady Ogilvy

The host should ascertain from the appropriate Royal Household whether any of these Members of the Royal Family will be present, and should notify guests accordingly if it is desired that decorations should be worn.

(b) At parties and dinners given in the houses of Ambassadors and Ministers accredited to the Court of St. James's, unless otherwise notified by the Ambassador or Minister concerned. An order, decoration or medal of the country concerned should be worn in preference to a British one, or should take precedence before all British awards (for fuller direction, see Section 3).

(c) At official dinners and receptions, including Royal Navy, Army, and Royal Air Force dinners, dinners of City livery companies and public dinners. The word 'Decorations' on the invitation card will be the host's intimation that the occasion is an official one.

(d) On official occasions when the host is:-

HM Lord-Lieutenant of a county, when within his or her county
The High Sheriff of a county, when within his or her county
a Cabinet Minister
an ex-Cabinet Minister
a Knight, or Lady of the Garter
a Knight, or Lady of the Thistle
a Great Officer of State, or of HM Household
a Lord Mayor, or Mayor
a Lord Provost, or Provost

The word 'Decorations' on the invitation card will be the host's intimation that the occasion is an official one.

In the case of (b), (c), and (d) above, the host should decide whether the nature or importance of the occasion makes it appropriate for decorations to be worn and then issue instructions on the invitation cards:

● if it is desired that decorations are to be worn with full evening dress, the invitation card should state 'Evening Dress – Decorations'.

● if it is desired that decorations are to be worn with dinner jacket, the invitation card should state 'Dinner Jacket – Decorations'.

● if it is desired that miniature medals and badges *only* are to be worn with dinner jacket, the invitation card should state 'Dinner Jacket – Miniatures'.

Ladies are to wear their decorations according to the requirement given to male invitees.

Occasions when Orders, Decorations and Medals are *not* worn

● When attending an investiture, either as guest or recipient (recipients and guests in uniform wear medal ribbons only, which, in the case of recipients, should include that of the order or decoration being received).

● When attending Royal garden parties.

● When attending parades or ceremonies as a spectator, unless ordered to wear them.

● On greatcoats.

5. Order of Wear

Whenever orders, decorations and medals are worn it is essential that they are displayed according to their correct precedence. The established and official 'order of wear' applicable in the United Kingdom (and in certain countries of the Commonwealth and the Overseas Territories), is laid down by the authority of the Central Chancery of the Orders of Knighthood. From time to time the Central Chancery publishes amended and updated versions in *The London Gazette*. The 'order of wear' set out below is the latest available, published on 14 March 2003. It is reproduced in a slightly modified form, excluding medals which ceased to be awarded long ago and where surviving recipients would be an impossibility, but does include a complete listing of medals for war and campaign service whose place in the officially published list is only indicated by the general heading of 'Campaign Medals and Stars'.

● Non-campaign honours and awards that have ceased to be given are marked ⁺.

VICTORIA CROSS	VC
GEORGE CROSS	GC

British Orders of Knighthood and other Distinctions

Knight Companion / Lady Companion of the Most Noble Order of the Garter	KG/LG
Knight / Lady of the Most Ancient and Most Noble Order of the Thistle	KT/LT
⁺ Knight of the Most Illustrious Order of St. Patrick	KP
Knight / Dame Grand Cross of the Most Honourable Order of the Bath	GCB
Member of the Order of Merit	OM
Baronet's Badge	Bt
⁺ Knight Grand Commander of the Most Exalted Star of India	GCSI
Knight / Dame Grand Cross of the Most Distinguished Order of St. Michael and St. George	GCMG
⁺ Knight Grand Commander of the Most Eminent Order of the Indian Empire	GCIE
⁺ Lady of the Imperial Order of the Crown of India	CI
Knight / Dame Grand Cross of the Royal Victorian Order	GCVO
Knight / Dame Grand Cross of the Most Excellent Order of the British Empire	GBE
Member of the Order of the Companions of Honour	CH
Knight / Dame Commander of the Most Honourable Order of the Bath	KCB/DCB
⁺ Knight Commander of the Most Exalted Order of the Star of India	KCSI
Knight / Dame Commander of the Most Distinguished Order of St. Michael and St. George	KCMG/DCMG

⁺ Knight Commander of the Most Eminent Order of the Indian Empire   KCIE
Knight / Dame Commander of the Royal Victorian Order   KCVO/DCVO
Knight / Dame Commander of the Most Excellent Order of the
    British Empire   KBE/DBE
Knight Bachelor's Badge   [*No post-nominals*]
Companion of the Most Honourable Order of the Bath   CB
⁺ Companion of the Most Exalted Order of the Star of India   CSI
Companion of the Most Distinguished Order of St. Michael and St. George   CMG
⁺ Companion of the Most Eminent Order of the Indian Empire   CIE
Commander of the Royal Victorian Order   CVO
Commander of the Most Excellent Order of the British Empire*   CBE
Companion of the Distinguished Service Order   DSO
Lieutenant of the Royal Victorian Order   LVO
Officer of the Most Excellent Order of the British Empire*   OBE
Companion of the Imperial Service Order ⁺   ISO
Member of the Royal Victorian Order   MVO
Member of the Most Excellent Order of the British Empire*   MBE
⁺ Indian Order of Merit (Military)   IOM

Decorations

Conspicuous Gallantry Cross   CGC
Royal Red Cross (1st Class)   RRC
Distinguished Service Cross   DSC
Military Cross   MC
Distinguished Flying Cross   DFC
Air Force Cross   AFC
Royal Red Cross (2nd Class), Associate   ARRC
⁺ Order of British India   OBI
⁺ Kaisar-i-Hind Medal (1st to 3rd Classes)
Order of St. John: Bailiff / Dame Grand Cross
        Knight / Dame of Justice
        Knight / Dame of Grace
        Commander (Brother / Sister)
        Officer (Brother / Sister)
        Serving Brother / Sister

---

* Same position for Gallantry awards of the Order
† No longer awarded in the United Kingdom

Medals for Gallantry and Distinguished Conduct

⁺ Union of South Africa Queen's Medal for Bravery (Gold)
⁺ Distinguished Conduct Medal DCM
⁺ Conspicuous Gallantry Medal CGM
⁺ Conspicuous Gallantry Medal (Flying) CGM (F)
 George Medal GM
⁺ Queen's (or King's) Police Medal, for Gallantry QPM/KPM
 Queen's Fire Service Medal, for Gallantry QFSM
⁺ Royal West African Frontier Force Distinguished Conduct Medal DCM
⁺ King's African Rifles Distinguished Conduct Medal DCM
⁺ Indian Distinguished Service Medal IDSM
⁺ Union of South Africa King's/Queen's Medal for Bravery (Silver)
⁺ Distinguished Service Medal DSM
⁺ Military Medal MM
⁺ Distinguished Flying Medal DFM
⁺ Air Force Medal AFM
⁺ Constabulary Medal (Ireland)
 Medal for Saving Life at Sea (Sea Gallantry Medal) SGM
⁺ Indian Order of Merit (Civil) IOM
⁺ Indian Police Medal for Gallantry
⁺ Ceylon Police Medal for Gallantry
⁺ Sierra Leone Police Medal for Gallantry
⁺ Sierra Leone Fire Brigades Medal for Gallantry
⁺ Colonial Police Medal, for Gallantry CPM
 Queen's Gallantry Medal QGM

Royal Victorian Medal (Gold) RVM
Royal Victorian Medal (Silver) RVM
Royal Victorian Medal (Bronze) RVM
British Empire Medal*† BEM

Queen's Police Medal, for Distinguished Service QPM
Queen's Fire Service Medal, for Distinguished Service QFSM
Queen's Volunteer Reserves Medal QVRM
Queen's Medal for Chiefs

---

* Same position for Gallantry awards of the Medal
† No longer awarded in the United Kingdom

Campaign Medals and Stars

1914 Star with dated 'Mons' clasp '5 Aug. – 22 Nov. 1914'
1914 Star
1914-15 Star
British War Medal
Mercantile Marine Medal
Victory Medal
Territorial Force War Medal

* India General Service Medal [1908-35]
* Naval General Service Medal [1915-62]
* General Service Medal [Army and RAF, 1918-62]
* India General Service Medal [1936-9]

1939-45 Star
Atlantic Star
Air Crew Europe Star
Africa Star
Pacific Star
Burma Star
Italy Star
France and Germany Star
Defence Medal
Canadian Volunteer Service Medal
1939-45 War Medal
1939-45 Africa Service Medal of the Union of South Africa
India Service Medal
New Zealand War Service Medal
Southern Rhodesia Service Medal
Australian Service Medal

Campaign Medals and Stars: Medals that appear against the marginal lines should always be worn in the order given. Those marked with a star(*) are positioned on the medal bar according to the date of participation in the *earliest* campaign recorded on the medal. International medals, such as those of the United Nations and NATO, are interspersed with the recipient's British campaign medals according to the date of participation in the mission for which individual medals have been awarded. A full list of campaign medals, each with the campaign clasps awarded with it, is given in Appendix 1. United Nations, NATO and other international medals are listed in Appendix 2.

Korea Medal 1950-53
Africa General Service Medal (Kenya 1952-6)
∗ General Service Medal 1962-
Vietnam Medal 1964-73
South Atlantic Medal 1982
Gulf Medal 1990-1
∗ Operational Service Medal 2000-
Iraq Medal 2003

United Nations Medals
NATO Medals
Multinational Force and Observers Medal (Sinai) 1982
European Community Monitoring Mission Medal (Yugoslavia) 1991
Western European Union Mission Service Medal 1994

Polar Medals (in order of date)
Imperial Service Medal

Police Medals for Valuable Service

⁺ Indian Police Medal for Meritorious Service
⁺ Ceylon Police Medal for Merit
⁺ Sierra Leone Police Medal for Meritorious Service
⁺ Sierra Leone Fire Brigades Medal for Meritorious Service
Colonial Police Medal for Meritorious Service   CPM

Badge of Honour

Coronation, Jubilee and Royal Household Medals

King George V's Silver Jubilee Medal, 1935
King George VI's Coronation Medal, 1937
Queen Elizabeth II's Coronation Medal, 1953
Queen Elizabeth II's Silver Jubilee Medal 1977
Queen Elizabeth II's Golden Jubilee Medal, 2002

King George V's Long and Faithful Service Medal
King George VI's Long and Faithful Service Medal
Queen Elizabeth II's Long and Faithful Service Medal

Long Service and Efficiency Decorations and Medals

Meritorious Service Medal (awarded to members of all Armed Forces from 1 Dec.
 1977, previously to the Army)
Accumulated Campaign Service Medal
Medal for Long Service and Good Conduct (Military)
Naval Long Service and Good Conduct Medal
⁺ Indian Army Long Service and Good Conduct Medal (European personnel)
⁺ Indian Army Meritorious Service Medal (European personnel)
Royal Marines Meritorious Service Medal
Royal Air Force Long Service and Good Conduct Medal
⁺ Medal for Long Service and Good Conduct (Ulster Defence Regiment)
⁺ Indian Long Service and Good Conduct Medal (Indian personnel)
⁺ Royal West African Frontier Force Long Service and Good Conduct Medal
⁺ Royal Sierra Leone Military Forces Long Service and Good Conduct Medal
⁺ King's West African Rifles Long Service and Good Conduct Medal
⁺ Indian Meritorious Service Medal (Indian personnel)
Police Long Service and Good Conduct Medal
Fire Brigade Long Service and Good Conduct Medal
⁺ African Police Medal for Meritorious Service
Royal Canadian Mounted Police Long Service Medal
⁺ Ceylon Police Long Service and Good Conduct Medal
⁺ Sierra Leone Police Long Service Medal
Colonial Police Long Service Medal
⁺ Sierra Leone Fire Brigades Long Service Medal
⁺ Mauritius Police Long Service and Good Conduct Medal
⁺ Mauritius Fire Services Long Service and Good Conduct Medal
⁺ Mauritius Prisons Service Long Service and Good Conduct Medal
Colonial Fire Brigades Long Service Medal
Colonial Prison Service Medal
⁺ Hong Kong Disciplined Services Medal

⁺ Army Emergency Reserve Decoration	ERD
⁺ Volunteer Officers' Decoration	VD
⁺ Volunteer Forces Long Service Medal	
⁺ Volunteer Officers' Decoration (for India and the Colonies)	VD
⁺ Volunteer Long Service Medal (for India and the Colonies)	
⁺ Colonial Auxiliary Forces Officers' Decoration	
⁺ Colonial Auxiliary Forces Long Service Medal	
⁺ Medal for Good Shooting (Navy)	
⁺ Militia Long Service Medal	
⁺ Imperial Yeomanry Long Service Medal	
⁺ Territorial Decoration	TD
⁺ Ceylon Armed Services Long Services Medal	
⁺ Efficiency Decoration	ED

⁺ Territorial Efficiency Medal
⁺ Efficiency Medal
⁺ Special Reserve Long Service and Good Conduct Medal
⁺ Decoration for Officers of the Royal Naval Reserve   RD
⁺ Decoration for Officers of the Royal Naval Volunteer Reserve   VRD
⁺ Royal Naval Reserve Long Service and Good Conduct Medal
⁺ Royal Naval Volunteer Reserve Long Service and Good Conduct Medal
⁺ Royal Naval Auxiliary Sick Berth Reserve Long Service and Good
    Conduct Medal
⁺ Royal Fleet Reserve Long Service and Good Conduct Medal
⁺ Royal Naval Wireless Auxiliary Reserve Long Service and Good
    Conduct Medal
  Royal Naval Auxiliary Services Long Service and Good Conduct Medal
⁺ Air Efficiency Award   AE
  Volunteer Reserves Service Medal
⁺ Ulster Defence Regiment Medal   UD
  Northern Ireland Home Service Medal
  Queen's Medal (for Champion Shots of the Royal Navy and Royal Marines
  Queen's Medal (for Champion Shots of the New Zealand Naval Forces)
  Queen's Medal (for Champion Shots in the Military Forces)
  Queen's Medal (for Champion Shots of the Air Forces)
  Cadet Forces Medal
  Coastguard Auxiliary Service Long Service Medal (formerly Rocket Apparatus
    Volunteer Long Service Medal, later Coast Life Saving Corps Long
    Service Medal)
  Special Constabulary Long Service Medal
  Canadian Forces Decoration   CD
  Royal Observer Corps Medal
  Civil Defence Long Service Medal
  Ambulance Service (Emergency Duties) Long Service and Good
    Conduct Medal
  Royal Fleet Auxiliary Service Medal

  Rhodesia Medal (1980)

⁺ Royal Ulster Constabulary Service Medal
  Northern Ireland Prison Service Medal

Independence Commemoration Medals

  Union of South Africa Commemoration Medal
  Indian Independence Medal (1947)
  Pakistan Medal (1947)

Ceylon Armed Services Inauguration Medal
Ceylon Police Independence Medal (1948)
Sierra Leone Independence Medal (1961)
Jamaica Independence Medal (1962)
Uganda Independence Medal (1962)
Malawi Independence Medal (1964)
Fiji Independence Medal (1970)
Papua New Guinea Independence Medal (1975)
Solomon Islands Independence Medal (1978)

Service Medal of the Order of St. John
Badge of the Order of the League of Mercy (*awards prior to June 1947*)
Voluntary Medical Service Medal
Women's Royal Voluntary Service Medal
South African Medal for War Service
Colonial Special Constabulary Medal

Honorary Membership of Commonwealth Orders (instituted by the Sovereign as Head of State of the Commonwealth Country, in order of date of award).

Other Commonwealth Members' Orders, Decorations and Medals (instituted since 1949 otherwise than by the Sovereign, including awards by States of Malaysia and Brunei, in order of date of award).

Foreign Orders   In order of date of award.

Foreign Decorations   In order of date of award.

Foreign Medals   In order of date of award.

Honours and awards which are not included in the Order of Wear:

The Royal Victorian Chain
Royal Family Orders

The four 'fourth level' awards have their own order of precedence, as follows:

Mention in Despatches
Queen's Commendation for Bravery
Queen's Commendation for Bravery in the Air
Queen's Commendation for Valuable Service

Life-saving medals for which the Sovereign's permission has been granted to wear on the *right* breast:

Royal Humane Society Stanhope Gold Medal
Royal Humane Society, Silver and Bronze Medals
Royal National Lifeboat Institution Medal (Gold, Silver, Bronze)
Order of St. John of Jerusalem Life Saving Medal (Gold, Silver, Bronze).

6. The Orders of Knighthood and other Insignia: general principles for wear

This Section introduces the principal rules and practices for wearing the various items of insignia belonging to the Orders of Knighthood and for wearing other insignia. The badges of the Fourth and Fifth Classes of Orders (LVO, MVO, OBE, MBE) and all other decorations worn as breast medals (including miniatures) are treated separately in the next Section.

Collars and Badges Appendant

● *Occasions when Collars are worn.*   The collars of the Orders of Knighthood are worn only at major state ceremonial occasions (such as the State Opening of Parliament), by those taking part in the introductions of peers and peeresses in the House of Lords (and who are entitled to wear the collar of one of the Orders), at the religious services of the Orders of Knighthood, and on other important occasions by Royal command.   Collars are only worn with ceremonial uniform, morning dress, peers' robes, and with the mantles of the Orders to which they belong.   The practice of wearing collars at Court on set 'Collar Days' has long since ceased to be observed.

● *Method of wearing.*   Only one collar may be worn at any given time.   This should be the senior if the wearer is entitled to two or more (unless, of course, he or she is habited in the robes of their less senior Order).   The collar is placed over the shoulders, as near as possible to the extreme point of each shoulder, and should hang down equally at the front and back, with the Badge suspended just below the front centre.

● *Collar Badges.*   The collars of the Orders of the Garter, the Thistle and the Bath have their own badges, but those of GCMG, GCVO and GBE do not; thus when one of the latter Collars is worn, the badge must be detached from the sash and attached to the collar.   There is no collar for the Order of St. John.

● *Collars and Sashes.*   If the collar of an Order is worn with uniform, the sash and badge of the same Order may not be worn; if the wearer possesses more than one Order, the sash of the next senior one should be worn.

Sashes (Broad Ribands) and Badges

● *Method of Wear.*   The sash (broad riband) of an Order is only worn with ceremonial uniform, full evening dress and full mess dress.   The sashes of the Garter and the Thistle are worn over the left shoulder, with the bow and badge on the right hip; the sashes of GCB, GCMG, GCVO, GBE and of the Order of St. John are worn over the right shoulder with the bow and badge resting on the left hip. (Rules for 'evening dress sashes' will be found in Sections 8 and 9.)

● *Sash Widths.* Gentlemen's sashes are of 102mm (4 ins.) width, except for the GCVO which is 95mm (3¾ ins.). Ladies' sashes for the Garter and the Thistle are 102mm (4 ins.) wide, and 57mm (2¼ ins.) in respect of the other Orders.

● *Sashes and Collars.* The sash of an Order may not be worn if the collar of that Order is worn at the same time, but if the wearer has such insignia of more than one Order, the sash of the next senior Order should be worn. Only one sash may be worn at any time.

● *Sash Badges worn as Neck or Bow Decorations.* The sash badge of the Order of the Garter, the Thistle, of GCB, GCMG, GCVO, GBE and of the Order of St. John may be worn with dinner jacket as a neck decoration, and by ladies as a bow decoration.

Breast Stars

● *Position worn and numbers.* The stars of all British Orders, and those of most foreign orders, are worn on the left side below any mounted group of decorations and medals (or a single decoration or medal). They are worn according to precedence in specified formations, but the maximum number at any one time may never exceed four, and includes the stars of any foreign orders and any which are required to be worn on the *right* side. Various additional restrictions on the maximum number that can be worn apply in the case of different types of uniform and civilian dress.

● *Means of attachment.* The large flattened pin with which the reverses of breast stars are fitted should not be inserted directly through the material of the uniform or coat. The pin should instead be inserted through small material loops called 'beckets' which, being of the same material and colour, are stitched to the garment in the position in which the star is to be worn. The task of fixing beckets should be undertaken by a tailor who should ascertain their correct position during a fitting while the garment is on the wearer. This will ensure that when they are worn, stars (and also medal brooch-bars) are positioned correctly and are not lopsided. As an alternative, small pins will effectively serve the same purpose.

Neck Decorations (Gentlemen, and Ladies in uniform)

● *Full-size badges only.* On all occasions, badges which are worn at the neck must be full-size. Miniature badges are never worn at the neck. It is not permissible for full-size neck-badges that cannot be worn on account of the restriction on number to be worn with full-size decorations and medals on the medal bar.

● *Limitations on number.* Up to three neck-badges may be worn at any one time with ceremonial uniform, although in many cases restrictions to fewer numbers apply. One badge only may be worn at any time with civilian day or evening/mess dress. When one badge is worn it should be the senior to which the wearer is entitled, and when two or more are worn they are arranged in descending order of seniority.

● *The riband.* Neck-badges are suspended from miniature-width ribands (16mm or ⅝ in.) with most types of uniform and with all types of civilian dress. The full-size riband used at investitures is not worn again, but a length of miniature-width riband is supplied with the insignia.

● *Additional neck decorations.* At evening functions (with both civilian and military dress), where the restriction is to one neck decoration, the badge worn should be the senior to which the wearer is entitled. Entitlement to additional neck decorations is indicated by the inclusion of the appropriate miniature badge on the miniature brooch-bar. (See 'Miniature Badges, Decorations and Medals' pp. 48–50).

● *Neck decorations not represented in miniature.* The badges of the *Order of Merit*, the *Order of the Companions of Honour*, and the *Baronet's Badge*, being the senior neck decorations, are never represented in miniature and included on the miniature medal-bar. With this exception they are treated as any other neck-badge with regard to the rules on numbers of neck-badges which may be worn in any given order of dress.

● *Directions for wear: particular awards.*
    - The *Order of Merit* Badge should be worn with the letters "For Merit" to the front.
    - The Badge of the *Order of St. Michael and St. George* should be worn with its obverse to the front, displaying the image of the Archangel St. Michael trampling the figure of Satan.
    - The *Royal Victorian Chain*, despite its collar-like appearance, is treated as a neck-badge in relation to the number of neck-badges that may be worn with uniform and civilian wear. The Chain, if worn with ceremonial dress, does not debar the wearing of a collar. If it is worn with evening dress, no other neck decoration may be worn. It is never worn or represented in miniature form.

The Insignia of Knight Bachelor

● *The Neck-Badge.* On receiving the accolade of knighthood a gentleman is presented with the Knight Bachelor's Neck-Badge. This is worn on a miniature-width neck riband with day or evening wear.

● *Breast 'Star'.* Gentlemen may, if they choose, wear a larger, pin-fitted Badge in the position of a breast 'star' on occasions when stars are directed to be worn. With evening dress this option makes it possible for another neck decoration to be worn that would otherwise only be represented in miniature on the miniature medal-bar.

The Knight Bachelor's Breast Badge may be purchased from the Imperial Society of Knights Bachelor, or its manufacturers, Garrards. It should be emphasised, however, that the 'star' is an optional addition to the Knight Bachelor's insignia and does not carry the same obligation to be worn as do the stars of Knight Commander in the Orders of Knighthood.

● *Directions for wear.* Both the Neck-Badge and the Breast-Badge of Knight Bachelor may be worn together with uniform and evening dress, but not with morning dress, the regulations for which prohibit the wearing of a star and neck-badge of the same Order or award. The Badge's riband should be included with other 'ribbons' when worn with uniform. The Badge should also be worn in miniature on the miniature brooch-bar with other decorations and medals.

● *Precedence of insignia.* It should be borne in mind when wearing either or both items of insignia that the Knight Bachelor's Neck-Badge has seniority over all Third Class neck-badges (i.e. CB, CMG, CVO and CBE), but the Breast Badge or 'star' takes precedence *after* all other breast stars and immediately after that of KBE (but before the stars of the Order of St. John).

Ladies' Bow Decorations (CBE and above)

● *'Bow and tails'.* Ladies (other than those wearing uniform) wear the equivalent of a gentleman's neck-badge on a 'bow and tails' formation of the appropriate riband. It is attached to the left side of the dress below any medals and above any stars. The badge worn is always the full-size version, and the riband always of full-size width, regardless of whether the bow is worn with day or evening dress.

● *Limitations on number worn.* One full-size bow decoration only may be worn of the Third Class (Companion or Commander) of an Order, or higher. This must be the senior to which the lady is entitled. With evening dress, other bow decorations to which a lady may be entitled should be represented on the miniature bar with other medals. The OM and CH, in a special class of their own, are exceptions to this rule and are never worn in miniature.

● *Two types of bow decoration may be worn.* Ladies' bow decorations which come under the above-mentioned restriction are to be distinguished from the Fourth and Fifth Classes of the Orders of Knighthood (LVO, MVO, OBE and MBE) and other decorations presented to ladies in the form of bow decorations. A lady who has one bow decoration of each kind, for example a CMG and an OBE, may wear both with day dress, but only *if* she has no other decorations or medals. (See 'Ladies: Civilian Dress' pp. 70–71). This would not be possible, however, with evening dress. On these occasions, the full-size CMG would be worn, and above it, on a brooch-bar, the OBE would be worn in miniature alongside (and after) a miniature badge representing the CMG. Only if the OBE was worn with no other decorations would it be worn on a miniature bow. Ladies wearing two or more miniatures are required to wear them from straight ribands on a miniature brooch-bar.

● *Adaptation of bow decorations for neckwear.* Ladies who are members of the Armed Forces are usually required to wear their bow decorations of DBE, CB, etc., as neck decorations. Although ladies in uniform are invested with their badges of Dame Commander or Companion/Commander on a bow, their insignia is provided with a fitment enabling the badge to be adapted for wear as a bow or neck decorations as occasion requires.

7. Medals, Ribbons and Miniatures

This Section concentrates on issues concerning orders, decorations and medals which are worn suspended from short ribands on the upper left hand side of the chest. In the following sequence, it deals with: 1. Full-size medals (methods of wear, arrangement, bars and clasps, emblems, and foreign awards); 2. Ribbons and ribbon bars; and 3. Miniature decorations and medals.

Regulations and requirements which are relative in to particular branches of the Armed Forces are also treated under the heading for that service in Section 10.

1. Full-Size Medals

(i) Methods of wear

Orders, decorations and medals that are worn suspended from straight ribands on the left breast must be worn in a horizontal line, and should be mounted for wear in one of two ways: 'ordinary' style, or 'court' style (sometimes also referred to as 'royal' style). For those actively involved in the Armed Forces or engaged in other forms of government or public service at home or overseas the choice of style will in most cases be determined by the authorities concerned, and advice should be sought accordingly. In the Royal Household all liveried staff are required, when on duty, to wear their medals mounted in the 'court' style. In the Army, the policy for court mounting is, in the interest of uniformity, left to the discretion of regiments and their corps.

For individuals who do not operate under public auspices the choice of style will be a matter of personal preference.

Ordinary Style
Medals mounted in 'ordinary' style utilize a single 'brooch-bar', a metal bar to which the top part of each riband is attached with the medal hanging loosely. The brooch-bar has a pin the length of the bar on its reverse side.

● *Arrangement of medals.* Medals must be arranged on the bar according to the 'order of wear' shown in Section 5, **and with reference to the additional points of guidance set out below**. The senior award must be fully visible and nearest the centre of the chest. Up to five medals may be worn side-by-side without the medals overlapping. Brooch-bars are available in sizes of up to five riband widths, but can be adapted to suit individual requirements. The bar itself must be unseen, although the need to ensure that medal ribands appear on the brooch-bar with no intervening gaps

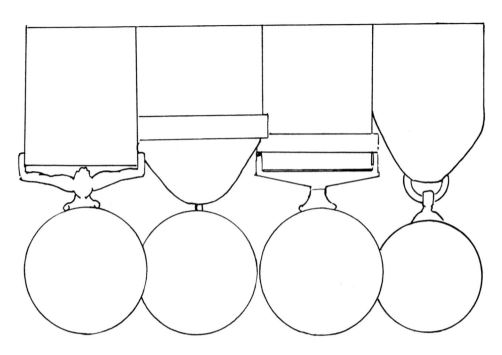

A group of 'ordinary' mounted medals.

will usually mean that there is some slight but unavoidable overlapping if medals or decorations exceed the breadth of the riband itself.

● *Overlapping.* With six medals or more it will be necessary for ribands, and therefore medals, to overlap. The degree of overlap will depend (i) on the number of medals, and (ii) on the individual's physique, but it should be equal for each riband. No maximum is laid down for the number of breast badges and medals that may be worn in this fashion. Regulations for the Armed Forces state that not more than two-thirds of a riband should be covered by the riband of an adjacent medal. Quantities of six or more medals requiring overlapping must be spaced evenly across the bar.

● *Obverse to the front.* Each medal must be worn with its 'obverse' showing frontwards. In many cases the obverse side will show the Sovereign's Head, Royal Cypher, or otherwise a crown, coat of arms, or national flag. Inscriptions, generally speaking, should be at the back (or 'reverse') of the medal.

● *Riband length.* Each riband, when mounted with its medal on the brooch-bar, should measure not less than 32mm (1¼ ins.) from the top of the riband to the top of the suspension or to the topmost clasp. When two or more medals and decorations are to be worn they should be arranged so that their lowest points are horizontally in line. Medal and decoration badges can vary in height, however, and Service regulations recognise that in order to allow a taller decoration to be suspended from a 32mm length of riband, adjacent medals are likely to require ribands of longer

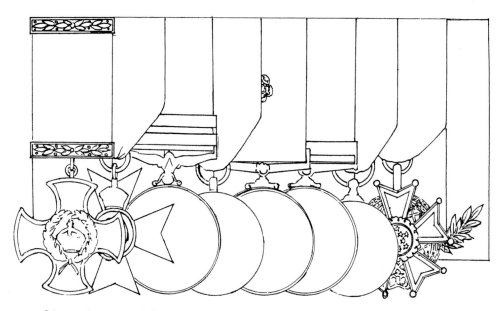

A group of 'court' mounted decorations and medals. The group commences with the breast decorations of DSO and LVO followed by the first campaign medal awarded (and containing a subsequent clasp). The Queen's Commendation emblem is shown mounted in last place, its correct position if no campaign medal is available for the theatre or zone of action in which it was awarded. The preceding decoration is a foreign award (United States Legion of Merit).

measurement. The addition of more than one clasp to a campaign medal will also necessitate longer ribands on accompanying medals.

Royal Navy. Riband lengths differ for personnel of the Royal Navy (see Section 10).

● *Awarded decoration or medal not received.* Medals and decorations which have been awarded but not yet received may still be represented on the medal-bar by the inclusion of a suitable length of the appropriate riband (usually the same length as the preceding one), correctly placed, among the other medals. This should only be done, however, if there is a specific requirement for medals to be worn on a particular occasion.

Court Style

Medals mounted in the 'court' style are mounted together in a rigid group. In contrast to medals mounted in the 'ordinary' style, decorations and medals mounted in this fashion are secured so that they do not make contact with each other and consequently avoid being chipped and scratched.

● *The court mounting method.* Each medal and its riband is mounted on to a buckram and cloth covered metal frame. The medal is held in position on the frame so that the riband measures 32mm (1¼ ins.) from the medal suspension, or topmost clasp, to the top of the frame. The riband then passes down the back of the covered frame and round to the front where it is brought up underneath the medal and sewn so that the area of frame showing beneath the medal is entirely covered with the riband. The medal is then stitched firmly in to place through the riband.

● *Size of frame.* The frame should be approximately 70mm (2½ ins.) in depth, extending downwards behind the medals to about one third of the distance from their aligned bottom edges. The lowest points of crosses, stars and medals must appear in a horizontal line. Service regulations state that the overall length of the suspended medal should be 89mm (3½ ins.). It is accepted, however, that the depth of the covered frame will depend on the height of the tallest decoration in the group, plus its 32mm (1¼ ins.) length of riband. The presence of a taller decoration and/or a medal with several bars or clasps will also increase the length of ribands required for accompanying medals on a mounted group. A metal brooch is sewn to the back of the covered frame for attachment to the uniform or coat.

● *Single decorations and medals.* It is permissible for a single decoration or medal to be court mounted.

'Beckets' and other means of attachment

When mounted medals are worn with uniform, the reverse pin is inserted through two or more 'beckets'. These are small loops of the uniform material which are sewn at equal distances horizontally in the position in which the medals are to be worn. Medals may also be attached by means of beckets when worn with civilian dress. It is essential that beckets are sewn correctly so that the brooch-bar, when worn on the garment, is horizontally level. Ideally, they should be sewn into position by a competent tailor. An alternative method is to align two safety pins on the inside of the garment so that the middle part of each pin is visible on the outside, creating a 'loop' through which the brooch-bar can pass, and enabling the medals to be held securely in position.

(ii) Arrangement of decorations and medals

Orders, decorations and medals must be arranged on the medal-bar in correct sequence according to their position in the 'order of wear'. The following notes provide additional points of guidance together with details of the regulations concerning bars, clasps and emblems.

Orders of Knighthood

Badges of the Orders of Knighthood are *not* worn on the medal-bar unless they are of a class required to be worn as suspended breast decorations, i.e. LVO, MVO, OBE and MBE. This prohibition applies also to the badges of OM and CH, to the Baronet's Badge, the Knight Bachelor's Neck Badge, and to the Order of St. John except its Fifth and Sixth Grade badges of Officer and Serving Brother/Sister which are breast decorations and may duly be included on the medal-bar.

Order of the British Empire

The OBE, MBE and BEM (Military and Civil Divisions) for Gallantry appear on the bar in the same 'order of wear' sequence for non-gallantry awards in the Order, i.e. an OBE (Civil) will appear before an MBE (Military) awarded for Gallantry. Awards in the Order which are of the same level, eg. an OBE (Military) and an OBE (Civil), should be arranged with the earlier award first.

Arrangement of campaign medals

Campaign medals are placed after any awards of the VC, GC, DSO, the Fourth and Fifth Classes of Orders, and other decorations and gallantry medals. They are arranged in date order of an individual's participation in a particular theatre, *not* the actual dates of the campaigns. The place of a General Service Medal or Naval General Service Medal with several bars among other campaign medals will thus be determined by the dates of participation in the zone of conflict recorded by the *first* bar on the medal.

- *International medals.*   UN, NATO and the medals of other international organisations which have been authorized for wear by British personnel take equal precedence with those medals instituted by the Crown, and are arranged with British medals according to the same rule of date of participation. Consequently, the first campaign medal in a group will be that which represents the recipient's earliest involvement in a zone of action, whether it is a British, UN or NATO medal.

- *World War II campaign stars and medals.*   The campaign stars of World War II form an exception to the above rule and are arranged in accordance with the sequence given in the official 'order of wear'.

Medals worn on the right side

Several medals of a non-military nature have the Sovereign's permission to be worn on the right side of the uniform or coat. These are:

Royal Humane Society Stanhope Gold Medal
Royal Humane Society, Silver and Bronze Medals
Royal National Lifeboat Institution Medal (Gold, Silver, Bronze)
Order of St. John of Jerusalem Life Saving Medal (Gold, Silver, Bronze)

They are worn on the *right* breast and in a corresponding position to any military medals worn on the left breast. Since these awards do not feature in the 'order of wear', if more than one is worn, they should be arranged in order of the dates on which the awards were made, the *earliest* being closest to the centre of the chest.

Bars and Clasps

Bars and clasps are terms which are sometimes used interchangeably, but in fact have separate meanings:

A *Bar* is a full-width metal device worn on the riband of a decoration or medal awarded for gallantry, bravery, distinguished or long service to denote the additional award of a particular decoration or medal. The bar to a decoration or medal is affixed to the riband, about a third of the way from the suspension. It is either sewn, or, if it has a 'back-strap', is slipped on to the riband.

A *Clasp* is a full-width metal device which records the geographical area or zone of a campaign and/or the period of a campaign, or additional periods of service. The first clasp is attached to the medal by means of lugs with rivet holes at both ends of the clasp through which the medal's suspender pin is passed and fixed. The next clasp is similarly attached to the one beneath, by means either of rivets or pins; thus the clasps are literally 'clasped' to the medal, rather than the riband. The first clasp earned is placed nearest the medal with each successive clasp being fitted according to the 'qualifying date', i.e. the date when the recipient entered an operational area. A list of clasps instituted for British campaign medals since 1914 can be found in Appendix 1.

- *World War II Campaign Stars.* Unlike other campaign awards, the 'clasps' for the World War II Stars are sewn to the riband, at just below the midway point. In respect of the *Atlantic Star, Air Crew Europe Star* and *France and Germany Star*, only one star could be awarded to an individual; a person who qualified for two wears the first star earned, with a clasp denoting the second star earned. Only one star and one clasp may be worn, even if the individual qualified for all three. A similar situation obtains in relation to the *Pacific Star* and the *Burma Star*, where an individual qualifying for both wears the star earned first with a clasp denoting the second.

- *Canal Zone 1951-4.* It should be especially noted that the clasp announced in October 2003 for service in the Canal Zone 1951-4, to be added to the Naval General Service Medal 1915 and the Army and RAF General Service Medal 1918, must be fitted in the correct chronological position among any other campaign clasps on those medals in accordance with an individual's dates of participation in the Suez campaign. It should not be added above clasps that record service of a later date.

Emblems

The term 'emblem' refers to devices of various designs which are affixed to the ribands of full-size medals, but which are not in the form of bars or clasps. Emblems are more usually worn on the 'ribbon strips' with undress uniform to denote the award of bars or clasps. They are also worn in miniature on miniature medals. Those which may be worn with full-size orders, decorations and medals are:

- *Order of the British Empire: for Gallantry* (OBE, MBE and BEM): a silver emblem of two crossed oak-leaves. If a bar has been added to the BEM, the Gallantry emblem is affixed above it.

- *South Atlantic Medal 1982*: this medal was given to all personnel who served in operations in the South Atlantic in 1982. A silver rosette is affixed to the centre of the ribbon in the case of recipients who saw at least one full day's service in the Falkland Islands or South Georgia, or 30 days in the operational zone.

- *Operational Service Medal (Sierra Leone 1999-2002)*: a silver rosette affixed to the centre of the riband is worn by personnel who took part in Operations Maidenly or Barras.

- *UN Medals*: silver Arabic numerals are affixed to the centre of the riband to denote the number of tours of duty on which a recipient has served in addition to the initial period of eligibility for the medal. Tour numerals may be worn on particular UN medals where authorisation has been given by the Defence Council.

- *NATO Medals*: bronze numerals denote additional tours of duty, and may be worn on those medals where the Defence Council has given authorisation. The numerals are affixed below the campaign bar on NATO medals; emblems denoting Mention in Despatches or the Queen's Commendation are affixed above it.

- *Multinational Force and Observers Medal*: a silver numeral is worn for additional tours of duty.

Mention in Despatches

These oak-leaf emblems are usually worn on the medal for the campaign in which the award was won. One emblem only may be worn on a General Service Medal, irrespective of the number of campaigns represented by the medal and its clasps in which an individual has been mentioned in despatches. However, single MiD emblems accruing from campaigns which have their own medals, may be worn on those different medals.

- *1914-19*: the emblem of bronze oak-leaves is worn on the riband of the Victory Medal. The award of this particular emblem ceased for deeds after 10 August 1920.

- *1920-39*: the bronze single oak-leaf emblem, if granted for service in operations between the two World Wars, is worn on the riband of the appropriate General Service Medal. If a General Service Medal has not been granted, the emblem is worn directly on the coat after any medal ribands.

- *1939-45*: the bronze single oak-leaf emblem is worn on the riband of the War Medal 1939-45. If the Medal has not been granted it is worn directly on the coat after any medal ribands.

- *1945-93*: the bronze single oak-leaf emblem is worn on the appropriate General Service Medal or campaign medal (including UN medals). If such a medal has not been granted, the emblem is worn directly on the coat after any medal ribands.

- *1993 onwards*: the silver single oak-leaf emblem for gallantry in active operations from 3 September 1993, if awarded for services in a theatre for which a campaign medal or clasp has been granted (including UN, NATO and WEU medals), is worn on the riband of the appropriate medal.

Sizes of emblem. There are three sizes of each emblem prior to September 1993: large, which is mounted on the full-size medal; medium, which is worn on the ribbon strip; and small, which is mounted on a miniature medal. For awards after September 1993, medium and small size emblems only are provided, the medium size being worn on both the full-size medal riband and the ribbon strip.

Method of wear. The Mention in Despatches emblem, when worn on a full-size campaign medal, should be affixed to the centre of the riband at an angle of 60 degrees from the inside edge of the riband, the leaf/leaves pointing upwards to the left shoulder. The emblem is placed *above* any clasp, or any other emblem or rosette on the appropriate medal riband. The emblem is worn at a lesser angle, or horizontally, only if the number of clasps and other emblems restricts the space available on the riband.

If the emblem is not worn on a campaign medal (as may be the situation if the award is for services out of the theatre or in a theatre for which no medal or clasp has been granted), the emblem is 'worn directly on the coat after any medal ribands'. The usual practice, however, if the wearer has other medals suspended from a brooch-bar, is for the emblem to be attached (by means of the emblem's reverse prongs) to a full-length strip of 'riband' matching the colour of the garment worn. Since the emblem does not have a place in the 'order of wear', it is mounted as the *last* item on the brooch-bar, after all British and foreign medals and decorations. The procedure is best undertaken when the other medals are mounted in court style; the strip of riband material extends from the top to the bottom of the frame, and the emblem should be placed near the bottom at the regulation 60 degree angle (see Illustration p. 37).

If, however, the wearer has no medals, the emblem is attached to the garment itself in the position that a single ribbon strip would occupy.

King's/Queen's Commendation emblems

- *King's / Queen's Commendation for Brave Conduct* (1939-94): for services during the 1939-45 War recipients wear a bronze single oak-leaf emblem (Armed Forces and Merchant Navy personnel) on the riband of the War Medal 1939-45; or a silver laurel-leaf spray (civilians) on the riband of the Defence Medal. Awards to military personnel after 1945 are affixed to the riband of the appropriate General Service Medal or campaign medal (including UN medals).

- *King's / Queen's Commendation for Valuable Service in the Air* (1939-94): for services during the 1939-45 War, Armed Forces personnel wear a bronze single oak-leaf emblem on the riband of the War Medal 1939-45, or subsequently on the riband of the appropriate General Service Medal or campaign medal (including UN medals). Civilians wear an oval silver badge on the coat immediately below any medals or medal ribands. In civil airline uniform the badge is worn on the central panel of the left breast pocket.

- *Queen's Commendation for Bravery* (1994 onwards): an emblem of silver laurel-leaves. When awarded for services in a theatre for which a campaign medal or clasp has been granted (including UN, NATO and WEU medals), it is worn on the riband of the appropriate medal.

- *Queen's Commendation for Bravery in the Air* (1994 onwards): this silver eagle emblem, when awarded to Armed Forces personnel, is worn as described for the Queen's Commendation for Bravery (1994 onwards).

- *Queen's Commendation for Valuable Service* (1993 onwards): this emblem of silver oak-leaves is worn as described for the Queen's Commendation for Bravery (1994 onwards).

Sizes of emblem. There are three sizes of each emblem prior to September 1993: large, which is mounted on the full-size medal; medium, which is worn on the ribbon strip; and small, which is mounted on a miniature medal. For the Queen's Commendation awards after September 1993, medium and small size emblems only are provided, the medium size being worn on both the medal riband and the ribbon strip.

Method of wear. When worn on a full-size campaign medal, the Commendation emblems are worn in exactly the same manner as described above for the Mention in Despatches emblem. It should be noted, however, that the QCBA silver eagle emblem is worn horizontally and not at a 60 degree angle. When no medal is available on which the emblem can be worn, but if the recipient has other medals, it may be mounted on a medal brooch-bar in the same manner as described above for the Mention in Despatches emblem. Having no position in the 'order of wear', it is likewise mounted at the end of the brooch-bar after all British and foreign decorations and medals. It is also in order for civilians who have received other official medals to wear a Commendation emblem in this manner.

When worn by civilians with no other medals, the emblem is affixed directly to the coat in the position that a single medal ribbon would occupy.

More than one emblem. Recipients of the emblems of Mention in Despatches and the Queen's Commendations are permitted to wear on a single medal riband one emblem only of each category of award. These should appear in the following order of precedence, beginning at the top of the medal riband:

> Mention in Despatches
> The Queen's Commendation for Bravery
> The Queen's Commendation for Bravery in the Air
> The Queen's Commendation for Valuable Service

The same precedence applies if there are no medals and the emblems are worn directly on the uniform or coat. In this case they are positioned horizontally in the position that a row of medal ribbons would occupy, with the MiD closest to the uniform buttons.

Foreign and Commonwealth decorations and medals

The insignia of foreign orders, decorations and medals are arranged on the medal brooch-bar in accordance with the 'order of wear'. It should be emphasised that where several awards have been received from each of several countries, the order of wear does not permit them to be arranged in a strictly country-by-country sequence. In the first instance awards must follow the sequence: Commonwealth (where the Sovereign is Head of State), Commonwealth (where the Sovereign is not Head of State), and Foreign. Within each of these categories awards are grouped into orders, then decorations, then medals. Each of these award-types is separately arranged into country groupings, two or more items received from one country being placed together in order of seniority. The country order, within each award-type, is determined by the date of bestowal of the *senior* award received from each country; the country of the earliest award is placed first.

- *Emblems and rosettes.* A feature that many foreign orders do not share with those of the United Kingdom is the circular ribbon rosettes that usually highlight a distinction between breast decorations of different classes. Rosettes must be kept entirely visible on a mounted medal-bar and it may be necessary, where ribands and medals overlap, to reposition the rosette so that it is not partially covered by adjacent ribands.

- *'Restricted wear' awards.* Commonwealth and foreign awards in the form of breast decorations that are subject to a 'restricted wear' stipulation should not, from a practical viewpoint, be mounted permanently in a medal group unless an individual is working or operating long-term within the donor country, in which case the decoration(s) should take precedence over British awards and occupy first place on the medal-bar. For more detailed direction on the wearing of foreign awards, see Section 3.

(iii) Ladies' decorations and medals

The rules for ladies who hold the Fourth and Fifth Class insignia of the Orders of Knighthood (i.e. LVO, MVO, OBE and MBE) and all decorations and medals of descending seniority, are virtually the same as those applicable to gentlemen. The principal difference is that ladies receive certain decorations and medals on 'bow and tails' or simple bow formations of the riband. Generally speaking, bow ribands accompany the more senior decorations, while most medals are received on straight ribands.

A lady who is the holder of a single decoration on a bow may wear it in that fashion on the left side, just below shoulder level, in the position of a medal-bar. If, however, a bow decoration, such as an OBE, is to be worn with one or more other medals, it must be converted to a straight riband and mounted with the other decorations/medals on a medal-bar in the same manner as for gentlemen. This requirement applies regardless of whether the lady is in uniform. (It is no longer permissible to wear an OBE or RRC on a bow and tails either mounted together with other medals, or in any other manner separately alongside mounted medals). Ladies who are members of the Armed Forces or of the Police, will in any case usually receive on a straight riband any decoration that would normally be presented to a lady on a bow.

Should a lady not wish to despoil the bow decoration which she has received at investiture, a 'replacement' or duplicate can be obtained from a supplier and be mounted for wear with other medals.

2. Ribbons and Ribbon Bars

Ribbon strips are widths of riband which are worn alone to signify the orders, decorations and medals which the wearer has received. They are usually worn with uniform, and are placed above the left breast pocket. They may also be worn on all occasions with all forms of civilian dress at the discretion of the wearer.

Types of ribbon bar. Medal ribbons may be sewn on to strips of buckram or similar material and then stitched on to the uniform or coat; or they may be sewn on to a brooch pin, allowing them to be detached from the coat or uniform as required.

Excepted ribbons. All British orders, decorations and medals may be represented on the ribbon bar with the exception of the *Orders of the Garter* and *the Thistle*, and the two *Baronets' Badges* (UK and Nova Scotia). Foreign awards for which an individual has 'restricted' permission to wear should also be excluded from the bar, unless a person is serving in the donor country for an extended period of time, in which case the appropriate ribbon or ribbons should be placed *before* those of British awards.

Arrangement. Ribbons are arranged side-by-side in strict accordance with the 'order of wear' with no gaps showing and no overlapping. Dress regulations concerning the number of ribbons that may be worn in each row differs between each of the Armed Services, and guidance on this score should therefore be sought under the appropriate headings of Section 10.

- *Order of the British Empire.* As noted earlier, it is possible for an individual to hold two classes in the Order simultaneously, one in each of the Military and Civil Divisions. In these circumstances the variant ribbons for both awards are worn, that for the higher class taking precedence over the lower. Both the BEM, and Gallantry awards of the Order/BEM, may also be held separately and irrespective of any other award(s) in the Order. The question of which ribbon(s) should appear on the ribbon bar is determined on the principle that no ribbon should exactly replicate one that is already present. Hence, the ribbon of a BEM (Military) should be omitted if there is also an MBE (Military), but should be included if either award is for Gallantry (and accordingly bears the Gallantry oak-leaves emblem). In the latter instance, a third ribbon of the Order would be required if the wearer was subsequently awarded an OBE (Civil), the three ribbons appearing in order of precedence, not in date order of bestowal.

Dimensions of ribbons.   The depth of ribbons (i.e. from top to bottom) should measure 13mm. (½ in.) for the Royal Navy; 9.5mm (⅜ in.) for the Royal Marines and the Army; and 11mm. (⁷⁄₁₆ in.) for the RAF.   Ribbon widths should be as specified for individual decorations and medals.

In respect of the Orders of Knighthood (as also the Order of St. John), membership of any class is denoted by a ribbon which is the width of that used for the *lowest* class of the Order concerned.   Thus an award of KCB (Military), for example, where the full-size neck riband is 51mm. (2 ins.) wide, is indicated on an officer's uniform ribbon bar by a ribbon strip of 38mm (1½ ins.) width, this being the width of riband for the CB. In the same way, a CBE, the riband of which is of 45mm (1¾ ins.) width, is denoted by a ribbon of 38mm (1½ ins.) width, this being the width of riband from which an MBE is suspended.   Full details of ribbon widths for the Orders of Knighthood are given in Appendix 3.

● *Armed Services:* Detailed regulations respecting the arrangement and positioning of medal ribbons on uniforms are explained under the headings for each of the Services in Section 10.

Ribbons worn on the right breast.   The ribbons of medals normally worn on the *right* breast are likewise worn on the right side of the uniform or coat, and in a corresponding position

Commencement of wear.   The appropriate medal ribbon may be worn with immediate effect from the date of the official announcement of an award in *The London Gazette*, in the case of orders, decorations for gallantry, and foreign awards, or from the date of receiving official confirmation of a campaign award, even though there will in most instances be some lapse of time before the insignia or medal is actually received.

Ribbon Bar Emblems

Emblems of various kinds are attached to medal ribbons, usually to denote instances where bars have been awarded in respect of a particular decoration or medal, or (in some recent instances) to signify the wearer's presence in a specific zone of operation during a campaign.   The ribbons for the following decorations and medals bear emblems as follows:

● The *Victoria Cross* and the *George Cross*: recipients wear a miniature replica of the cross in the centre of their ribbon strip.   A bar to either decoration is indicated by the addition of a second miniature cross.   These small replica crosses are not worn on the full-size riband.

● The *Order of the British Empire (Gallantry)*: awards for gallantry (OBE, MBE and BEM) are denoted by a silver crossed oak-leaf emblem.

● *The British Empire Medal.*   A bar to the BEM (Civil or Military) is denoted by a silver rosette.   If the original BEM was a Gallantry award, the rosette is situated next to the Gallantry emblem, the latter being placed farthest from the left shoulder.

● The *Order of St. John of Jerusalem*: a miniature silver version of the Maltese cross is worn on the centre of the black ribbon by recipients of all Grades of the Order. Its purpose is to distinguish the ribbon against a dark background.

● Gallantry decorations and medals, and long service and good conduct medals: holders of these awards who receive bars for subsequent acts of bravery, or to indicate further periods of service, wear a centrally-placed silver rosette on the ribbon strip.

● WWII campaign stars: the single bar permitted for each campaign star is represented on the ribbon strip by a silver rosette, the exception being the *1939-45 Star* where the 'Battle of Britain' bar is represented by a gilt rosette. Servicemen entitled to the *Africa Star* with a bar for their role with the 1st or 8th Armies wear either a silver numeral '1' or '8' on the ribbon.

● General Service Medals: the campaign clasps to these medals are *not* represented on the appropriate ribbons.

● Campaign medals: clasps (or rosettes) to certain medals for specific parts of campaigns or operations are represented on the ribbon by silver rosettes: the *South Atlantic Medal*, the *Gulf Medal*, the *Operational Service Medal (Sierra Leone, for Operations Maidenly and Barras)*, the *Iraq Medal*.

● UN and NATO medals: tour of duty numerals are centrally affixed to ribbons, silver for UN medals, bronze for NATO medals.

● *Mentions in Despatches* and *Queen's Commendations*: the medium-size emblems for these awards are worn on the appropriate ribbons. If an emblem is not associated with a particular campaign medal, it is worn on a ribbon of usual width and depth, and should match the colour of the uniform on which it is stitched. Since these emblems do not have a place in the 'order of wear', they must be mounted as the *last* item in a set of ribbons. In the absence of any ribbons the emblem is worn in the position in which a single ribbon would occupy. The oak-leaf and laurel-leaf emblems, normally placed at a 60 degree angle on the full medal riband, should be placed horizontally across the ribbon, the stalk furthest from the left shoulder.

More than one emblem. When a silver rosette is worn on a ribbon with either an MiD or Queen's Commendation emblem, the rosette is placed farthest from the left shoulder and the emblem is placed horizontally alongside it. Since there is only sufficient space on the ribbon for one emblem, a person who is entitled to include more than one emblem on the full-size medal wears whichever is the senior on the ribbon strip in accordance with the order of precedence for emblems, as follows:

Mention in Despatches
Queen's Commendation for Bravery

Queen's Commendation for Valuable Service in the Air
Queen's Commendation for Valuable Service

Rosettes - Foreign awards.   In the case of some foreign orders the rosette on the ribbon strip may be embellished with metallic coloured 'wings' or 'flashes' projecting from either side in order to signify a particular class of an order. Additionally, a version of the rosette can be worn in the buttonhole with everyday dress. The system of rosettes and 'wings' often employed with European orders is generally as follows, although it should be noted that there are many variations.   A recipient intending to add the ribbon of an order to his or her ribbon bar is advised, in cases of uncertainty, to ascertain the correct emblem, if any, by contacting the embassy or high commission of the country concerned.

1st class, Grand Cross	all gold
2nd class, Grand Officer/Commander 1st Class	half gold, half silver
3rd class, Commander	all silver
4th class, Officer	rosette only
5th class, Knight	plain ribbon, no rosette

3.   Miniature Decorations and Medals

Miniature orders, decorations and medals are exact replicas of their full-size counterparts, and are worn on a miniature brooch-bar by ladies and gentlemen with evening and mess dress. The items worn in miniature are those decorations and medals that are worn on the full-size medal-bar (or any unmounted single item). Miniature badges are also worn to signify membership of a British or foreign order of a higher class or grade than would be worn as a breast decoration, either singly or on a brooch-bar (see 'Orders of Knighthood' below). Decorations, medals and their ribands are half the size of the full-size versions. All other insignia, such as stars and neck-badges, are without exception worn in their full-size state.

In the United Kingdom miniatures are not included with the full-size insignia or medals with which a recipient is invested or receives, and must be separately purchased from a supplier.

● *Orders of Knighthood.*   Miniature badges that denote membership of one or more of the Orders of Knighthood at the level of Third Class (Companion or Commander), or higher, are permanently included on the miniature brooch-bar and are worn regardless of whether the related full-size insignia are also worn. Thus a gentleman who is a KBE (or a lady who is a DBE) will wear the full-size insignia, and will wear the miniature badge of the Order of the British Empire on the brooch-bar, provided they have other orders, decorations or medals which can also represented (see below, however, 'When miniatures may not be worn').

The rule, originally promulgated by King George V in 1923, is that the respective badges must be half the size of the badge of the *lowest* class in each Order. The *Order of St. John* also follows this rule; and the *Knight Bachelor's Badge* is likewise worn in miniature with its riband on the medal-bar. Ribands, in common with those of all other miniatures, are of a uniform 16mm (⅝ in.) width.

● *Insignia not worn in miniature.* The following insignia are never represented in the form of miniature badges:

> The Order of the Garter
> The Order of the Thistle
> The Order of Merit
> The Order of the Companions of Honour
> Baronet's Badge
> The Royal Victorian Chain

● *Precedence.* Miniature orders, decorations and medals must appear on the medal-bar in accordance with their position in the 'order of wear'. It is important that badges for the Orders of Knighthood are arranged according to the particular Class they represent. In the case of a gentleman with a KBE and CVO, for example, the enamel badge for the Order of the British Empire will come before that for the Royal Victorian Order. This situation does not apply to the Order of St. John whose grades are grouped together and take precedence *after* the principal decorations.

● *When miniatures may not be worn.* Insignia of the Orders of Knighthood of the level of Third Class (Companion or Commander), or higher, may not be worn in miniature if the wearer is in possession of only one such award, i.e. if a CBE Neck-Badge is being worn and is unaccompanied by any other orders, decorations or medals, British or foreign, a miniature badge representing the CBE may not also be worn. The miniature can be worn, however, if there is one or more other orders, decorations or medals which can be worn with it on the miniature brooch-bar. The miniature of a single Fourth or Fifth Class breast badge (LVO, MVO, OBE or MBE), or of any other decoration or medal, is not affected by this rule and may be worn by itself.

● *Mounting.* Miniature decorations and medals may be mounted and worn either in the 'court' style or the 'ordinary' style. Badges and medals are suspended from ribands of a width of 16mm. (⅝ in.). The length of the brooch should not normally exceed 14.7 cm. (5¾ ins.), i.e. nine miniatures not overlapped, but a larger number of miniatures may necessitate a longer brooch. The bottom edges of mounted miniatures should be aligned and not exceed 57 mm (2¼ ins.) from the top of the riband to the lowest point of the miniature insignia. The lengths of each individal riband displayed will consequently vary according to the height of each Order badge, decoration and medal. The number of clasps or bars attached to the riband of any miniature may require that ribands across the whole brooch be of additional length.

● *Bars and Emblems.*   Any bars or emblems displayed on the full-size medals must be displayed in miniature in their corresponding positions on miniature decorations and medals.

● *Foreign awards.*   Foreign awards are worn subject to the rules governing permission to wear in 'restricted' and 'unrestricted' circumstances (see Section 3).

● *Ladies' miniatures.*   Ladies may wear on a miniature brooch-bar any orders, decorations and medals to which they are entitled. The brooch-bar (or single miniature decoration or medal) is worn on the left side in the upper shoulder area and above any bow decorations.   All Order badges, decorations and medals are suspended from straight ribands.   Thus a lady who has a CBE and an LVO will wear the miniature badge of the Order of the British Empire on a straight riband, followed by that for her LVO plus any other medal to which she is entitled; her full-size CBE decoration will be worn below the medal brooch-bar.
   A miniature Fourth or Fifth Class badge (LVO, MVO, OBE or MBE), when not worn with any other medals is worn on a miniature riband bow (as also is any other single decoration which in its full-size state is worn from a bow), but if worn with other medals the decoration badge or medal must be suspended from a straight miniature riband and mounted with the other medals on a brooch-bar.

8. Gentlemen: Civilian Dress

There are four styles of civilian dress with which gentlemen wear insignia: Full Evening Dress, Dinner Jacket, Morning Dress and Lounge Suit.

Full Evening Dress ('White Tie')

On occasions when gentlemen are required to wear orders, decorations and medals with Full Evening Dress, invitations to guests should state, 'Evening Dress – Decorations'. Insignia are worn in the following manner:

● The Collar of an Order of Knighthood is not worn.

1. The Sash (Broad Riband) and Badge
Gentlemen should wear the broad riband and badge of the senior Order which they hold, with the star of the same Order taking precedence before the stars of any other Orders.

The broad riband is worn under the tailcoat and over the waistcoat. It is a shortened version of the full-length riband and does not pass over the shoulder and down the back of the body.   The shortened riband should be tailored to fit the body correctly, and the top edge fashioned to avoid sagging. The riband has two buttonholes at the far end of the longer, 'display' section which are fastened to two buttons situated at the front of the left or right armhole of the waistcoat.   The riband passes diagonally across the front of the waistcoat, and the other, short end of the riband, shaped into a point and having a buttonhole, connects with a button situated at the lower side of waistcoat.   This enables the bow and badge to rest on the right hip (Garter, Thistle), or on the left hip (GCB, GCMG, GCVO, GBE, Bailiffs Grand Cross, Order of St. John), and to be clearly visible at the right or left 'cutaway' side of the tailcoat.

2. Breast Stars
A maximum of four stars may be worn. They should be positioned on the left side of the tail coat below the breast pocket.   A single star should be placed centrally over the heart.   If two or more stars are to be worn, they should be arranged symmetrically according to their position in the 'order of wear', in one of the following formations (looking at the wearer), and so that they are not touching:

Two Stars	Three Stars	Four Stars
1	1	1
2	2 3	2 3
		4

Gentleman's Full Evening Dress. The broad riband and badge of the senior Order to which the gentleman is entitled (in this case the Garter) is worn with the maximum number of four breast stars (in this case the stars of KG, GCMG, GCVO and Knight of Justice, Order of St. John), and the neck decoration (Order of St. John). Membership of these Orders (with the exception of the Garter) is denoted by miniature badges on the brooch-bar together with the MC and other medals.

Any combination of stars may be worn in these formations, the general sequence being stars of the Orders of the Garter and of the Thistle, the stars of Knight Grand Cross, the stars of Knight Commander, the Knight Bachelor's Breast Badge or 'star' (if worn), the stars of the Order of St. John, and, where appropriate, the stars of any foreign orders. Stars should ideally be attached to the coat in their correct positions by means of beckets.

- *Knight Bachelor's Breast Badge.* A gentleman who is a Knight Grand Cross or Knight Commander of an Order is entitled, if he has been promoted from the rank of Knight Bachelor, to wear his Knight Bachelor's Breast Badge or 'star' with the star of his subsequent award.

3.   The Neck-Badge

One neck decoration only may be worn with Full Evening Dress. The badge is suspended from a miniature width riband, fastened at the back with a 'hook and eye'. The riband should fit neatly around the lower edge of the collar of the shirt (emerging at either side from under the neck band of the white tie) and below the collar 'wings' and the tie, so that the badge hangs centrally with the top of the suspension ring no more than 25mm (1 in.) below the tie knot.

- *The 'seniority' rule.* The badge worn should always be the senior insignia that the wearer is entitled to wear as a neck decoration. The OM, CH, the Baronet's Badge, or the Royal Victorian Chain take precedence over all other neck decorations and, unlike other badges, are not represented on the miniature brooch-bar. Thus if a gentleman is the holder of more than one of these particular awards, he will wear whichever is his senior badge, but unfortunately may not represent his next senior award in any fashion. If a gentleman is a CH and a Knight Commander of one of the Orders, he should wear the Knight Commander's star and the CH badge. On the other hand, if he is a KCMG and CB, he should wear the KCMG Star and its related Neck-Badge, and include the badges for both Orders with any other medals on his miniature brooch-bar. If a gentleman is a CH and is also a Knight Bachelor, CVO and CBE, he is obliged to wear the CH, this being his most senior neck decoration, and represent his other three neck-badges in the usual form on the miniature bar. Being precluded from wearing the Knight Bachelor's Neck-Badge, he does, of course have the option of wearing the Knight Bachelor's 'breast star'. This latter expedient enables Knight Bachelors who hold other awards of the level of Companion or Commander to wear whichever neck decoration they may hold next in order of seniority.

4.   Miniature Decorations and Medals

The miniature badges of all orders, decorations and medals, British and foreign, which a gentleman is entitled to wear are displayed in their correct sequence on a miniature brooch-bar. The brooch-bar is situated approximately midway between the breast pocket opening and the point of the left lapel. If necessary, a longer brooch may extend leftwards on to the shoulder area of the coat and be partly attached there. However, the bar must not extend beyond the shoulder seam, nor beyond the inner edge of the left lapel.

Badges that denote membership of an Order at the level of Companion or Commander, or higher, are permanently included on the bar and are worn regardless of whether the full-size insignia itself is worn. A Knight Bachelor continues to wear the appropriate miniature badge on his brooch-bar if he subsequently becomes a Knight Commander or Knight Grand Cross of an Order of Knighthood.

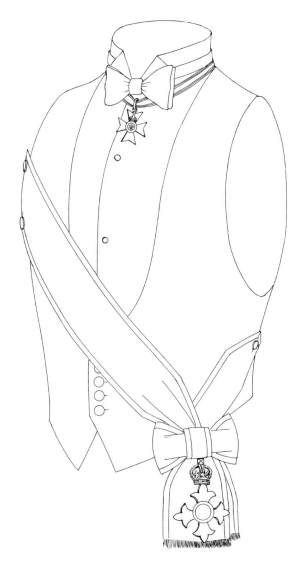

Gentleman's Full Evening Dress. The method of attaching the broad riband (sash) and badge to the waistcoat underneath the tailcoat of the Full Evening Dress.

● *Exception to the wearing of miniature badges.* A miniature badge denoting membership of an Order at the level of Companion or Commander, or higher, is *not* worn if the gentleman has no other orders, decorations or medals to represent on a miniature brooch-bar. Thus if a gentleman is a KCB but has no other orders, decorations or medals, either British or foreign, he does not wear a miniature badge for the KCB. This rule does not apply, however, to the Fourth and Fifth Class badges of Orders (i.e. LVO, MVO, OBE, MBE, plus the equivalent Grades of the Order of St. John, and of foreign orders), which being breast decorations may be worn singly in miniature if necessary. A miniature of any other decoration or medal may likewise be worn on its own.

5. Foreign Orders, Decorations and Medals.

Generally speaking, gentlemen who have 'unrestricted' permission from the Sovereign to wear foreign awards, may do so at any function where Full Evening Dress is worn, the insignia taking precedence *after* British insignia. However, at a function in honour of the Head of State of a foreign nation, or a representative, holders of official awards of that nation will wear them in a manner that gives them precedence *before* their British awards.

Gentlemen who have 'restricted' permission to wear foreign insignia do not wear them with British insignia *unless* they are attending a function specifically in honour of the nation from which they have received the award. Thus persons with only 'restricted' permission in respect of their foreign awards should not include them in a permanent position on their miniature brooch-bar.

The protocol and regulations governing the wearing of foreign insignia are fully explained in Section 3.

Dinner Jacket ('Black Tie')

On occasions when gentlemen are required to wear orders, decorations and medals with Dinner Jacket, invitations to guests should state, 'Dinner Jacket – Decorations'. Insignia are worn in the following manner:

● The Collars and Sashes of Orders of Knighthood are not worn.

1. The Breast Star
One star only may be worn and should be positioned centrally on the left side of the jacket. The star should be the most senior to which the gentleman is entitled.

2. The Neck-Badge
One neck-badge only may be worn. The full-size neck decoration is worn on a miniature-width riband. With an upright 'wing' collar the riband fits around the outside of the collar, and with a soft downturned collar it is worn underneath the collar. It is fastened at the back with a 'hook and eye'. The top of the badge's suspension ring should be no more than 25mm (1 in.) below the knot of the tie. The badge should be the senior to which the gentleman is entitled (for further direction on this point, see above under 'Full Evening Dress').

    ● *Sash Badges worn as Neck Decorations*. When the star is worn of a Knight of the Garter, or Knight of the Thistle, or of GCB, GCMG, GCVO, GBE or of Bailiff Grand Cross of the Order of St. John, the accompanying sash badge of the Order may be worn as a neck decoration. The badge is transferred from the sash and is worn from a riband of the usual miniature width. In the event that a gentleman holds two or more of these honours, he should wear the star of the senior Order, and the full-size badge of the second Order. (Bailiffs Grand Cross of the Order of St. John wear a smaller version of the sash badge.) This regulation should be considered as

Dinner Jacket. This shows the new regulation whereby a Knight Grand Cross of an Order (in this case that of GCMG) wears his sash badge as a neck decoration. The appropriate miniature is worn with miniatures of the LVO, OBE and other medals.

mandatory unless, however, a gentleman holds any other neck decoration by virtue, for example, of his being a Baronet, a Member of the Order of Merit, a Companion of Honour, a Knight Commander, Knight Bachelor or a Companion/Commander of another Order, when he should wear whichever is the senior of these neck decorations with his Garter, Thistle or Grand Cross star. It should be noted, however, that this regulation applies *only* to those occasions on which gentlemen wear Decorations with Dinner Jacket, and, of course, does not apply to foreign orders.

● *Knight Commanders* of the Orders of Knighthood, unless they hold one of the senior neck decorations (such as the OM or CH), should wear the breast star of their Order with the related neck-badge.

● *Knight Bachelor's Badge.* As explained in the rules for Full Evening Dress, the Knight Bachelor's Badge may be worn either at the neck, or in a larger version as a breast 'star'. The latter option allows a Third Class (Companion or Commander) neck-badge to be worn. It is also permissible, however, for the Knight Bachelor's Neck-Badge and Breast-Badge to be worn at the same time.

3. Miniature Decorations and Medals
The miniature badges of all orders, decorations and medals, British and foreign, which a gentleman is entitled to wear are displayed in their correct sequence on a miniature brooch-bar. The brooch-bar, or single decoration or medal, should be situated on the lapel at a level of an inch or so below the point of the left lapel. For further direction, see above under 'Full Evening Dress'.

4. Foreign Orders, Decorations and Medals
The wearing of foreign insignia with Dinner Jacket is subject to the regulations summarised above under 'Full Evening Dress' and detailed in Section 3. Any foreign insignia worn with Dinner Jacket are comprehended within the usual restrictions on insignia on these occasions.

Morning Dress

Insignia are worn with Morning Dress on only a few occasions during the public calendar, such as important Royal celebrations, religious services of the Orders of Knighthood, and memorial services for nationally prominent figures. The organisers of an official occasion or public event at which Morning Dress is ordered to be worn should also indicate whether the wearing of orders, decorations and medals would be appropriate.

● The Broad Riband of an Order is not worn.

1. The Collar
The collar of an Order of Knighthood may be worn with Morning Dress, but only when specifically required. In the event that the wearer holds the collar of more than one Order, the senior should be worn. The collar, with its badge appendant, should be placed over the shoulders, as near as possible to the extreme point of each shoulder, and should hang down equally at the back and front, the badge suspended just below front centre. It should be fastened at the shoulders by black thread or gold safety pins.

2. The Breast Star
On most occasions one star only may be worn, and should be positioned centrally on the left side of the coat below the medal brooch-bar or any single decorations or

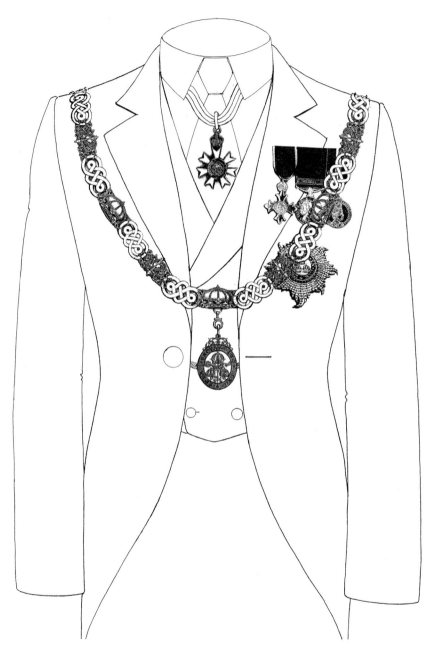

Morning Dress.   The collar and breast star of GCB (Civil) are worn, together with the neck decoration of CMG, and the breast decoration of OBE with other medals. The GCB Collar would not normally be worn unless specially ordered for a State occasion.

medals.   This should be the senior star to which a gentleman is entitled.   In exceptional circumstances, and where specially directed, the limit is increased to allow up to four stars to be worn. They should be arranged in the manner laid down for Full Evening Dress.

3. The Neck-Badge
One neck decoration only may be worn, this being the senior to which the wearer is entitled. It is suspended from a miniature width riband worn under the shirt collar, with the top of the badge's suspension ring at 25mm (1 in.) below the knot of the tie, the badge itself resting on the front of the tie.

- *Knight Commanders* of the Orders of Knighthood *do not* wear with Morning Dress the neck-badge that belongs with the star of the Order they are wearing. This will mean that they can only wear a neck decoration at all if they have received another award that comprises a neck decoration. If they choose, Knight Commanders (or Knights Grand Cross) who are former Knight Bachelors may wear their Knight Bachelor's Neck-Badge.

- *Knight Bachelors* do not wear both the Knight Bachelor's Neck-Badge and Breast-Badge with Morning Dress. If they choose not to wear the breast star, they are obliged to wear their Neck-Badge, this badge having precedence over all Third Class (Companion or Commander) awards in the Orders of Knighthood. Ideally, however, a Knight Bachelor who also holds a Third Class neck decoration of an Order should wear this together with the Knight Bachelor's Breast Badge or 'star'.

4. Decorations and Medals
A mounted group of full-size decorations and medals, or a single medal or decoration, may be worn on the left side of the coat. The top of the medals should be positioned at buttonhole level with the bottom points of the medals slightly above the breast pocket. The medal-bar may, if warranted by its length, cross the lapel and come up to, but not go beyond the inner edge of the lapel.

5. Foreign Orders, Decorations and Medals
Foreign insignia may be worn with Morning Dress in the circumstances and manner explained in Section 3.

Lounge Suit

There are some day-time occasions, such as Remembrance services, Regimental or Veterans' functions, at which those attending are required to wear decorations and medals with lounge suits.

- Collars, Broad Ribands and Breast Stars are not worn.

1. The Neck-Badge
One neck decoration only may be worn. It should be the senior to which the holder is entitled. The badge is suspended from a miniature width riband which is worn under the shirt collar, with the top of the badge's suspension ring at 25mm (1in.) below the knot of the tie, the badge itself resting on the front of the tie.

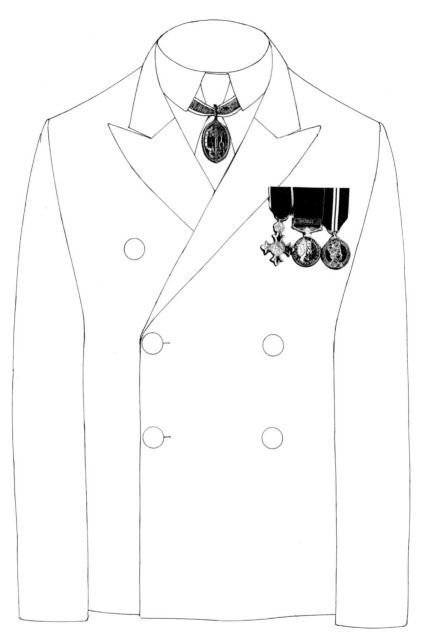

Lounge Suit.   The neck-badge of Knight Bachelor is worn, the OBE is mounted with other medals on a brooch-bar.   Breast stars are not worn with lounge suits.

● *Knight Commanders.* If a gentleman's senior award is that of Knight Commander of an Order, he may wear the neck-badge, but not the associate star. However, a gentleman who is, say, a GCMG and has no other award that is of itself, or includes, a neck decoration, will wear only his medal brooch-bar or any single breast decorations or medals.

2. Decorations and Medals

A mounted group of full-size decorations and medals, or a single decoration or medal, may be worn on the left side of the jacket. The top of the medal(s) should be positioned at buttonhole level with the bottom edges of the medals just above the breast pocket. The medal-bar may, if warranted by its length, be brought up to the inner edge of the lapel. When full-size medals are worn with lounge suit, the jacket should be buttoned. At similar evening functions when lounge suits are worn, miniature orders, decorations and medals may be worn together with any neck decoration to which the wearer is entitled.

3. Foreign Orders, Decorations and Medals

Foreign insignia may be worn with Lounge Suit in the circumstances and manner explained in Section 3.

Overcoats

Only full-size orders, decorations and medals which are mounted on a brooch-bar may be worn with overcoats. They are worn in the usual fashion on the left side. At Remembrance parades neck-badges may be worn at the discretion of the holder. Breast stars and other insignia are never worn.

9. Ladies: Civilian Dress

Ladies wear insignia at evening 'White Tie' or 'Black Tie' events, and with Day Dress when gentlemen wear decorations with Morning Dress or Lounge Suit.

Full Evening Dress ('White Tie' occasions)

On occasions when ladies are required to wear orders, decorations and medals with Full Evening Dress, invitations to guests should state, 'Evening Dress – Decorations'. Insignia are to be worn in the following manner:

- The Collar of an Order of Knighthood is not worn.

1. The Sash Riband and Badge
Ladies should wear the sash riband and badge of the senior Order which they hold, with the star of the same Order taking precedence before the stars of any other Orders. The sash riband is 102mm (4 ins.) in width for Ladies of the Garter, and of the Thistle, and 57mm (2¼ ins.) for Dames Grand Cross of the other Orders. The full-length riband is worn, passing over the left or right shoulder, with the bow and badge resting on the right hip (Garter, Thistle), or the left hip (GCB, GCMG, GCVO, GBE, Dame Grand Cross, Order of St. John). The riband should, if possible, be attached to the dress at or near the shoulder to prevent it from slipping, and if necessary the bow should likewise be secured.

2. Breast Stars
A maximum of four stars may be worn. They should be positioned on the left side of the dress. A single star should be placed approximately 15cm (6 ins.) above the waist. If two or more are worn, they should be arranged according to their seniority in the following manner (looking at the wearer), so that they are not touching, and with the lowest star or stars placed approximately 15cm above the waist:

Two Stars	Three Stars	Four Stars
1	1	1
2	2 3	2 3
		4

Any combination of stars may be worn in these formations, the general sequence being stars of the Orders of the Garter and of the Thistle, the stars of Dame Grand Cross, the stars of Dame Commander, the stars of the Order of St. John, and, where appropriate, the stars of any foreign orders.

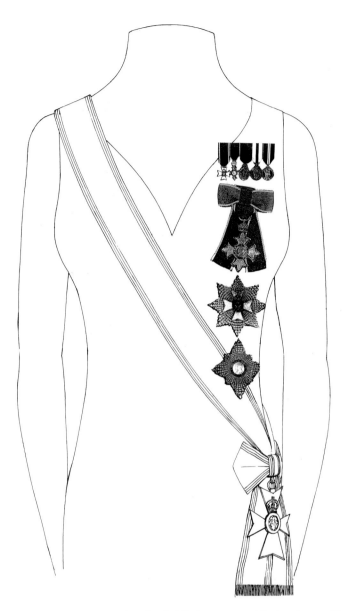

Lady's Full Evening Dress. The star and sash of GCVO is worn with the star and bow decoration of a DBE. These awards, and another bow decoration to which the lady is entitled (the CB), are represented in miniature with her other medals.

---

3. The Bow Decoration

Ladies may wear one full-size bow decoration. The full-size badge, which is mounted on a full-size bow formation of the appropriate riband, is worn on the left side of the dress above any stars. If a miniature brooch-bar is being worn the bow should be situated centrally below it. If a brooch-bar is not being worn, the bow decoration should be placed higher up in the front shoulder area on the left hand side of the dress.

• *The 'seniority' rule.*   The bow decoration worn should always be the senior which the lady is entitled to wear, i.e. Third Class (Companion or Commander) of an Order, or higher. Any additional such decorations (of this level or higher) are represented on the miniature brooch-bar. Thus, a lady who holds the CH and is also a DBE will be obliged to wear the CH as her bow decoration together with her DBE star, while a miniature badge representing the DBE is included on the brooch-bar. (Neither the OM or CH are represented in miniature form). If, on the other hand, a lady is a DBE and a CMG, she will wear the DBE star and bow badge, and a badge representing her CMG will be included in miniature on the brooch-bar after that for the DBE.

4. Miniature Decorations and Medals

The miniature badges of all orders, decorations and medals, British and foreign, which a lady is entitled to wear should be displayed in their correct sequence on a miniature brooch-bar. The brooch-bar is worn on the left side of the dress in the upper shoulder area, and above any bow decoration. All decorations and medals should be suspended from straight miniature ribands, and none should appear on bows.

• *Exception to the wearing of miniature badges.*   A miniature badge denoting membership of an Order at the level of Third Class (Companion or Commander), or higher, is *not* worn if the lady has no other orders, decorations or medals to represent on a miniature brooch-bar. Thus if a lady is a DBE but has no other orders, decorations or medals, either British or foreign, she may not wear a miniature badge for the DBE. This rule does not apply, however, to the Fourth and Fifth Class badges of Orders (i.e. LVO, MVO, OBE and MBE, plus the equivalent Grades of the Order of St. John, and of foreign orders), which being breast decorations may be worn singly in miniature if necessary. A miniature of any other decoration or medal may likewise be worn on its own.

• *Single miniature badges.*   The miniature of a Fourth or Fifth Class award of an Order or other decoration should, if worn singly, be suspended from a miniature bow, but not if the lady is wearing Mess Dress.

5. Foreign Orders, Decorations and Medals.

Generally speaking, ladies who have 'unrestricted' permission from the Sovereign to wear foreign awards, may do so at any function where full evening dress is worn, the insignia taking precedence *after* British insignia. However, at a function in honour of the head of state of a foreign nation, or his or her representative, holders of official awards of that nation will wear them in a manner that gives them precedence *before* their British awards.

Ladies who have 'restricted' permission to wear foreign insignia do not wear them with British insignia *unless* they are attending a function specifically in honour of the nation from which they have received the award. Thus ladies with only 'restricted' permission in respect of their foreign awards should not include them in a permanent position on their miniature brooch-bar.

The protocol and regulations governing the wearing of foreign insignia are fully explained in Section 3.

Evening Dress ('Black Tie' occasions)

When ladies are required to wear orders, decorations and medals at 'black tie' events, invitations to guests should state, 'Dinner Jacket – Decorations'. Insignia are to be

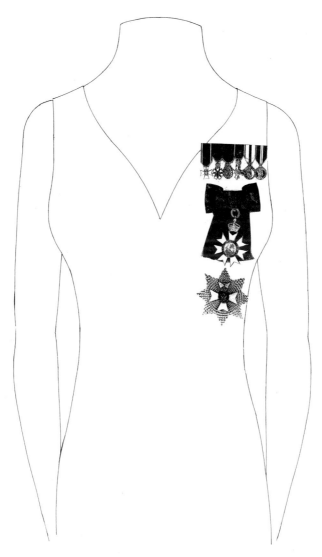

Lady, 'Black Tie' Occasion (1). This shows the maximum of insignia which may be worn, i.e. one breast star and one bow decoration (in this case the star of GCVO, with the bow decoration of a DCMG). These awards, and another bow decoration, which the lady is not wearing (the CB), are represented in their correct sequence with other medals on the miniature brooch-bar.

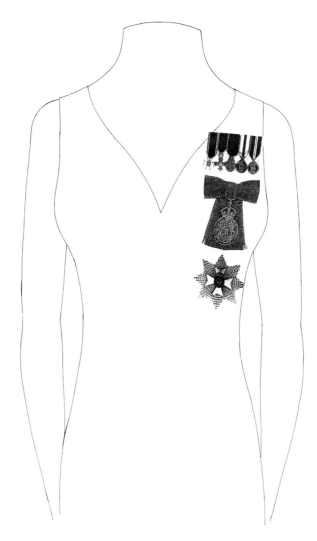

Lady, 'Black Tie' Occasion (2).   The star of GCVO is worn with the bow decoration of CH. Two other awards, those of DBE and CB, are represented on the miniature brooch-bar.   Neither the OM nor the CH is ever represented in miniature.

---

worn in the following manner:

● The Collars and Sash Ribands of Orders of Knighthood are not worn.

1.   The Star
One star only may be worn and should be positioned on the left side of the dress approximately 15cm (6 ins.) above the waist.   The star should be the senior to which the lady is entitled.

2.   The Bow Decoration
Ladies may wear one full-size bow decoration.   The full-size badge, which is mounted on a full-size bow formation of the appropriate riband, is worn on the left side of the

dress above any breast stars. If a miniature brooch-bar (or a single miniature decoration or medal) is being worn, the bow should be centrally positioned below it. If a brooch-bar is not being worn, the bow decoration should be placed higher up in the front shoulder area on the left side of the dress. The badge should be the most senior to which the lady is entitled (for further direction on this point, see under 'Full Evening Dress' above).

- *Sash badges worn as bow decorations.* When the star is worn of a Lady of the Garter, or Lady of the Thistle, or of GCB, GCMG, GCVO, GBE or of Dame Grand Cross of the Order of St. John, the accompanying sash badge of an Order may be worn as a bow decoration. The badge is transferred from the sash and is attached to a bow formation of the appropriate riband of 38mm (1½ins.) width. In the event that a lady holds two or more of these honours, she should wear the star of the senior Order, and the full-size badge of the second Order. (Dames Grand Cross of the Order of St. John wear a smaller version of the sash badge.) This regulation should be considered as mandatory unless, however, a lady holds any other bow decoration by virtue, for example, of her being a Member of the Order of Merit, a Companion of Honour, a Dame Commander, or a Companion/Commander of another Order, when she should wear whichever is the senior of these bow decorations with her Garter, Thistle or Grand Cross star. It should be noted, however, that this regulation applies *only* to occasions on which ladies wear Decorations at 'Black Tie' events, and, of course, does not apply to foreign orders.

- *Dame Commanders* of the Orders of Knighthood, unless they hold one of the most senior bow decorations, namely the OM or CH, should wear the star of their Order with the related full-size bow decoration.

3. Miniature Decorations and Medals

The miniature badges of all orders, decorations and medals, British and foreign, which a lady is entitled to wear should be displayed in their correct sequence on a miniature brooch-bar. The brooch-bar is worn on the left side of the dress in the upper shoulder area, above any bow decoration. For further direction see above under 'Full Evening Dress'.

4. Foreign Orders, Decorations and Medals

The wearing of foreign insignia at 'Black Tie' events is subject to the regulations summarised above under 'Full Evening Dress' and detailed in Section 3. Any foreign insignia worn at 'Black Tie' events are comprehended within the usual restrictions on insignia on these occasions.

Formal Day Dress (when Gentlemen wear Morning Dress)

When there is a requirement for gentlemen to wear decorations with Morning Dress, ladies should wear decorations in the equivalent manner with Day Dress. Such occasions include important Royal celebrations, religious services of the Orders of Knighthood, and memorial services for nationally prominent figures. The organisers

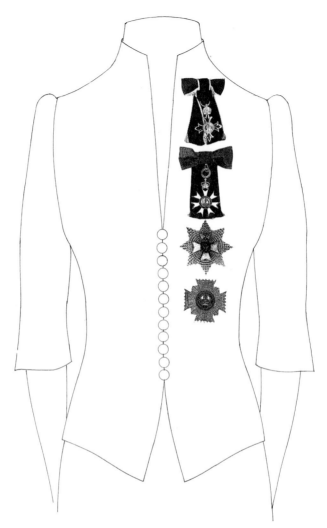

Lady's Formal Day Dress (1) (when gentlemen wear Morning Dress). The stars of GCVO and DCB are worn (in most cases one star only may be worn). Since regulations prohibit the wearing of the DCB bow decoration, the lady is wearing another bow decoration to which she is entitled, that of CMG. In the absence of other medals, the OBE is retained on its bow and is worn in the position a medal brooch bar would occupy.

---

of an official occasion or public event at which Morning Dress is ordered to be worn should also indicate whether the wearing of orders, decorations and medals would be appropriate.

● The Sash Riband of an Order is not worn.

1. The Collar

Ladies wear the collar of an Order of Knighthood when gentlemen are requested to wear theirs with Morning Dress, although such occasions are rare. The collar, with its badge appendant, should be placed over the shoulders, as near as possible to the

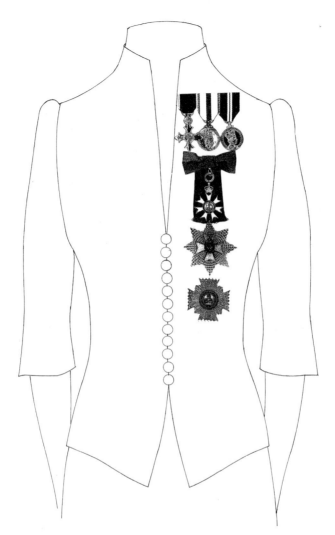

Lady's Formal Day Dress (2) (when gentlemen wear Morning Dress). This shows the same
layout of insignia as in the previous illustration, but with the OBE mounted and worn as a 'breast
decoration' with two other medals.

extreme point of each shoulder, and should hang down equally at the back and front,
the badge suspended just below front centre. It should be fastened at the shoulders
by gold safety pins or thread matching the colour of the coat.

2. The Breast Star
One star only is usually worn, centrally placed on the left side approximately 15cm
(6 ins.) above the waist. In exceptional circumstances and when specified, up to four
stars may be worn, the lowest of which, again, must be about 15cm above the waist.
They should be arranged according to the patterns prescribed for ladies' Full Evening
Dress (see above).

3. The Bow Decoration

Ladies may wear one full-size bow decoration of Companion or Commander of an Order, or higher. It should be the senior to which she is entitled. The full-size badge is mounted on a full-size bow formation of the appropriate riband and is worn on the left side above any star or stars, and if worn with full-size medals, below the medal-bar.

- *Dame Commanders* of the Orders of Knighthood *do not* wear with Day Dress the bow decoration that belongs with the star of the Order they are wearing. This will mean that they can only wear a bow decoration at all if they have received another award that comprises a bow decoration.

4. Decorations and Medals

A group of full-size decorations and medals suspended from straight ribands and mounted on a medal-bar, or a single full-size decoration or medal worn on either a bow or a straight riband, may be worn on the left upper shoulder area above any bow decorations.

- *Fourth and Fifth Class Badges (LVO, MVO, OBE, MBE) and other decorations.* Ladies who wish to wear these particular decorations with other full-size medals (including any others they may have received on a bow), must have the bows replaced with straight ribands and the medals mounted on a medal brooch-bar. If, however, a lady wishes to wear a single decoration only, she may wear it on its original bow mounting. It should be placed above any full-size bow decoration of the Third Class of Companion or Commander, or higher.

5. Foreign Orders, Decorations and Medals

Foreign insignia may be worn in the circumstances and manner explained in Section 3.

Day Dress (when Gentlemen wear Lounge Suit)

There are some day-time occasions, such as Remembrance services, Regimental or Veterans' functions, at which ladies attending are required to wear decorations and medals.

- Collars, Sash Ribands and Breast Stars are not worn.

1. The Bow Decoration

Ladies may wear one full-size bow decoration of Companion or Commander of an Order, or higher. It should be the senior to which she is entitled. The full-size badge is mounted on a full-size bow formation of the appropriate riband and is worn on the left side above any star or stars, and if worn with full-size medals, below the medal-bar.

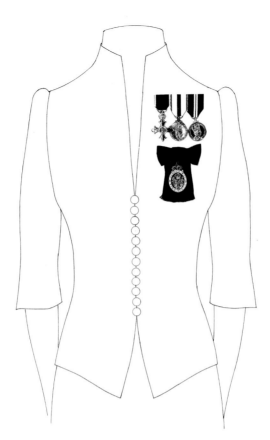

Lady's Day Dress. This shows the maximum of insignia permitted when gentlemen wear decorations and medals with lounge suits. Taking the previously shown example of a lady who is a GCVO, DCB, CMG and OBE, she would wear only her senior bow decoration (that of DCB), and her OBE mounted with other medals. The OBE would be worn on its bow in the absence of other medals.

● *Dame Commanders.*   If a lady's senior award is that of Dame Commander of an Order, she may wear the bow decoration, but not the associate star. However, a lady who is, say, a GBE and has no other award that is of itself, or includes, a bow decoration, will wear only her medal brooch-bar or any single decoration or medal.

2. Decorations and Medals

A group of full-size decorations and medals suspended from straight ribands and mounted on a medal-bar, or a single full-size decoration or medal worn on either a bow or a straight riband, may be worn on the left upper shoulder area above any bow decorations (for further direction, see above under 'Formal Day Dress'). At similar evening functions when Day Dress is worn, miniature orders, decorations and medals may be worn together with any full-size bow decoration to which the wearer may be entitled.

3. Foreign Orders, Decorations and Medals

Foreign insignia may be worn in the circumstances and manner explained in Section 3.

10. The Armed Forces

This Section concentrates on the requirements for wearing orders, decorations and medals with the uniforms of the Armed Forces.   Close attention has been paid to the current editions of Dress Regulations for the Royal Navy, the Army, and the Royal Air Force.   The approach adopted here has been to relate the regulation requirements as closely as possible to those uniforms on which insignia and medals are customarily worn, and for ease of use the Section is divided into three main parts, dealing with each service in turn and concluding with a final sub-section on Mess Dress.   In most cases, the accompanying illustrations do not show the absolute maximum of insignia which may be worn with each uniform, but instead demonstrate 'optimum' layouts that are more usually seen for the uniforms shown.

The mode of wearing certain items of insignia belonging to the Orders of Knighthood is essentially the same for the ceremonial uniforms of each of the three Services and is detailed separately below under the heading 'Collars, Broad Ribands and Stars'. Otherwise, the particular rules and requirements for the wearing of insignia and medals in respect of each Service are set out under the separate headings for the Royal Navy, the Army and the Royal Air Force.

Over the last decade or so the uniforms worn by women have been brought closely into line with those worn by men, hence the manner of wearing insignia and medals as described in this Section may be assumed to be applicable to both sexes except where indicated.

All matters concerning the medal-bar, ribbons and miniatures are separately covered in Section 7, although regulations and practices which are specific to a particular Service (such as the positioning of medal ribbons) are treated under the heading for that Service.

Preliminary Issues

Single and Joint Service Occasions.
Throughout this Section the regulation restrictions on insignia worn are given as for 'Single Service' occasions, but since the requirements for wearing insignia at 'Joint Service' events are substantially the same (and in fact only differ insofar as the number of neck decorations are concerned), the regulations given below may therefore be taken to apply both to Single *and* Joint Service events.   Where differences occur in respect of 'Joint Service' rules, these are indicated.

Foreign and Commonwealth honours.
Members of the Armed Services may wear with British insignia, any foreign insignia for which they have been granted 'unrestricted' permission.   In these circumstances

the insignia of foreign and commonwealth awards take precedence after all British honours.

There is usually a requirement to wear the insignia of a particular foreign nation at functions and events organised by, or in honour of, the head of state or representative of that nation, and will be applicable to personnel whether they have 'unrestricted' or 'restricted' permission to wear the insignia concerned.   On these occasions the appropriate broad riband, star, neck decoration, breast decoration or medal should be worn in 'pride of place' and take precedence over all equivalent British insignia.   The correct practice for the wearing of foreign insignia and medals is fully explained in Section 3.

Awards prior to enlistment.
A person enlisted in the Armed Forces who previous to enlistment has been awarded any order, decoration or medal listed in the Order of Wear (including foreign insignia granted unrestricted permission by the Sovereign), is entitled to wear the award with uniform, regardless of his or her status at the time of the award.   An ex-policeman, for example, who has been awarded the Queen's Police Medal, would be entitled to wear the medal ribbon, and on appropriate occasions the medal itself, with Service uniform.

Collars, Broad Ribands and Stars

The collars and sashes (broad ribands) of the Orders of Knighthood are worn only with the full ceremonial uniforms of the Services.   As the regulations for wear are the same for these uniforms in all three Services, they are treated separately in this subsection, as are the general rules regarding the positioning of breast stars.

The Collar and Badge

The Collar chain and its badge appendant is only worn on **'full ceremonial'** occasions when specifically ordered.   It is worn with the following Service uniforms:

- *Royal Navy.* Ceremonial Day Coat, and No. 1A Dress.
- *Army.* Full Dress, General Officers' Frock Coat, and No. 1 Dress (Ceremonial).
- *Royal Air Force.* No. 1A Dress.

One collar only may be worn, and if the wearer possesses more than one, it should always be that of the most senior Order.   The broad riband of the Order may not be worn at the same time.   The collar should be placed over the shoulders, as near as possible to the extreme point of each shoulder, and should hang down equally at the front and back, with the badge suspended just below the front centre.   The collar should pass under the shoulder boards, shoulder cords or shoulder straps of the uniform (where it is secured with small gold safety pins), and over the aiguillettes.

The Sash (Broad Riband) and Badge

The full sash riband and badge of an Order of Knighthood is worn only on **'full ceremonial'** occasions with the following Service uniforms:

- *Royal Navy*. Ceremonial Day Coat, and No. 1A Dress.
- *Army*. Full Dress, General Officers' Frock Coat, and No. 1 Dress (Ceremonial).
- *Royal Air Force*. No. 1A Dress.

An officer who possesses the broad riband of more than one Order will wear the senior one, unless he or she is wearing the collar, in which case if he or she has more than one Order, the broad riband of the next senior Order should be worn.

The riband should pass over the appropriate shoulder, but under the shoulder cord, shoulder board or shoulder strap, and fit diagonally across the body at the front and back. It is positioned under the aiguillette (and under the uniform lapel, where necessary), and should pass under the waist sash or waist belt, with the bow and badge resting on the left or right hip as appropriate. The ribands of the Orders of the Garter and Thistle pass over the left shoulder and rest on the right hip; those of the other British Orders (GCB, GCMG, GCVO, GBE, Order of St. John) pass over the right shoulder and rest on the left hip. On collar-wearing occasions, the collar rather than the riband of the senior Order is worn. The broad riband of the next senior Order is worn if the officer is in possession of one, but if not, he/she should wear only the collar, and not the riband.

- *Orders of the Garter, and of the Thistle*. Since the sashes of these Orders pass over the *left* shoulder, it may in some cases be necessary for breast decorations and medals to be positioned over the sash. Where a brooch-bar is of insufficient length to span the breadth of the riband, it should be affixed to beckets on the uniform through the material of the sash riband. For this purpose, it will be necessary to have two holes or cuts specially tailored at the correct level in the sash material which can be aligned with the uniform beckets beneath the sash, so that the brooch's pin can pass through.

Breast Stars

The stars of the British Orders of Knighthood, and most foreign orders, are worn on the left side below decorations and medals. The maximum number that may be worn on a **'full ceremonial'** occasion is four, but on a **'ceremonial day'** occasion the maximum is two. If one star is worn, it should be positioned on the left side centrally below the medal brooch-bar. If two or more stars are worn, they should be positioned according to their seniority and so that they are not touching, in the following formations (looking at the wearer):

Two Stars	Three Stars	Four Stars
1	1	1
2	2 3	2 3
		4

These formations apply both to day uniforms and evening/mess dress. Specific requirements in relation to Royal Navy, Army and Royal Air Force uniforms, and for Mess Dress, are detailed under these headings in the next sub-section.

The Royal Navy

1.   Ceremonial Day Coat, No. 1A Dress and No. 1AW Dress
The *Ceremonial Day Coat* is worn on **'full ceremonial day'** occasions by Admirals of the Fleet, Admirals, and other authorised officers.   Otherwise, the *No. 1A Dress*

Royal Navy – Admiral's Ceremonial Day Coat.   The Breast Star, Broad Riband and Badge of GCB are worn with the neck decoration of CVO.   A second neck decoration (Commander, Order of St. John) is worn from a riband slip attached to the inside of the coatee between the third and fourth buttons. The breast decorations of OBE and DSC are mounted and worn with campaign and other medals.

('Reefer Jacket'), or the *No. 1AW Dress* (warm weather officers' white tunic) is worn on these occasions. Orders, decorations and medals are worn with these uniforms as follows:

(a) Collar and/or Broad Riband and Badge are worn as described above on pp. 73–74.

(b) Breast Stars
Ceremonial Day Coat.
Up to four stars may be worn, positioned as follows:
   One star: below the medal brooch-bar, to the left of the left-hand row of buttons, and equidistant between the lower edges of the medals and the waist belt.
   Two stars: one above the other, the second immediately and centrally below the first.
   Three stars: a triangular formation, the first star immediately and centrally below the medal brooch-bar, with stars two and three either side beneath. It may prove necessary for the second star to cover one or more of the left-hand buttons.
   Four stars: a diamond formation, essentially the above triangular arrangement but with the fourth star positioned centrally below, in vertical line with the first.

No. 1A Dress and No. 1AW Dress.
   One star: in the centre line of the breast pocket with the upper point not less than 25mm (1 in.) below the tip of the pocket.
   Two stars: the second aligned directly below the first, the upper point of the second star being not less than 25mm below the lower point of the first.
   Three stars: a triangular formation, the second and third stars side by side and centrally below the first, the second in seniority towards the wearer's right, the third on the left. Should this arrangement interfere with a broad riband passing from right shoulder to left hip, there are two options: (i) officers of the Royal Navy are permitted to invert the triangular arrangement of the stars so that the first and second are worn side by side, the senior star to the wearer's right, with the third star centrally beneath; or, (ii) the bow of the riband can be brought forward a little to rest on the front of the hip, thus allowing more space on the left side for the stars.
   Four stars: a diamond formation, the first star in the centre line of the breast pocket, the second and third either side below (the second towards the wearer's right); and the fourth centrally beneath again and in vertical line with the first.

● When either three or four stars are worn with No. 1A Dress it is necessary to position the first so that the second is not touching the top left-hand button of the coat. To avoid this, Navy regulations permit the first star to be worn with its topmost point up to 13mm (½ in.) above the lip of the breast pocket.

(c) Neck Decorations
A maximum of three neck decorations may be worn with the Ceremonial Day Coat

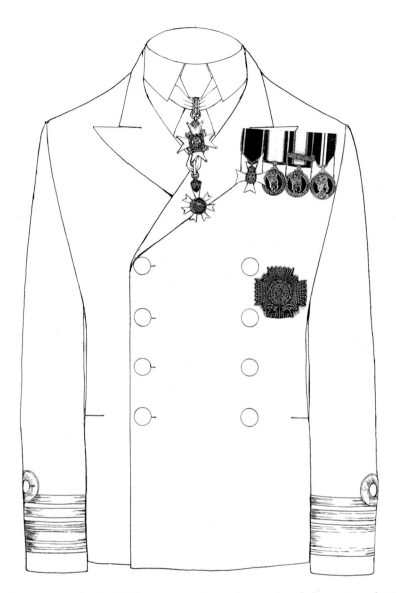

Royal Navy – Vice-Admiral's No. 1A Dress. The Breast Star and neck decoration of KCB is worn with a second neck decoration, that of CMG. The breast decoration of LVO is worn with other medals.

(two on 'Joint Service' occasions), and two with No. 1A or No. 1AW Dress on 'full ceremonial day' occasions. The badges are worn in descending order of seniority, beginning with Knight Commanders' badges, then those of Companion and/or Commander.

Ceremonial Day Coat. The first badge is worn on a miniature width riband attached to the inside of the collar and emerging between the collar's connecting hook and eye and the bottom of the collar itself. A second badge, if worn, is suspended from a 76mm (3 ins.) length of riband attached by a hook to a small eye stitched inside the coat and emerging between the first and second buttons on the *right-hand* side of the coatee.   A third neck-badge is similarly attached, the riband emerging between the second and third buttons.   (If, however, a GCB or GBE sash riband is worn with this uniform, thus covering over the area in which the badges should be attached, a second neck-badge may be worn from a riband slip emerging from the inside of the coatee on the *right* side, below the position of the sash, between the third and fourth buttons.)

No. 1A Dress.   The first badge is worn on a miniature width riband around the neck under the shirt collar (or short length of riband attached to the underside of the collar points), with the top of the badge's suspension ring immediately below the knot of the tie.   A second neck-badge is suspended immediately below the first, resting on the cross of the lapel, its riband attached by a hook to the inside of the shirt.

No. 1AW Dress (officers' white tunic).   The first badge is worn on a riband attached to the inside of the tunic collar and emerging under the collar's lower hook and eye. A second neck-badge is suspended from a short riband attached by hook and eye to the inside of the tunic midway between the first and second buttons.

(d) Single Medals/Medal Brooch-Bar

A single full-size decoration or medal, or mounted group of full-size medals, should be worn on the left side of the uniform coat.   Decorations and medals should be mounted in accordance with the directions in Section 7.

Ceremonial Day Coat.   The medals should be situated centrally on the left side and on a level just below the top left-hand button of the uniform.

No. 1A Dress and No. 1AW Dress.   The medals are worn immediately above the top row of medal ribbons sewn to the garment; or in the same position, and using the same beckets, as the top row of detachable ribbons (see 'Medal Ribbons' below).   If the medals are to be worn on garments on which medal ribbons are sewn, care must be taken to ensure that the ribbons are completely covered.   The medal-bar may, if necessary, come over the lapel, but should not project outward beyond the shoulder, or inward beyond the opening of the coat.   When a rifle is carried by Warrant Officers and Senior Ratings, the medal brooch-bar may be partially covered by the lapel as a protection for the medals.

2. No. 1B Dress and No. 1BW Dress

The *No. 1B Dress* (or its warm weather equivalent, *No. 1BW Dress,* which may comprise the officers' white tunic) is worn on **'ceremonial day'** occasions.   Mounted groups of full-size medals, or single decorations and medals are worn, and officers may wear a maximum of **two** breast stars and **one** neck decoration.   These insignia are positioned in the manner described above as for the *No. 1A Dress* on 'full ceremonial' occasions.   No other insignia may be worn.

3. Full-size Decorations and Medals
Both Officers and Ratings may wear their decorations and medals mounted either in 'court style' or 'ordinary style' at their own option.

Naval uniform regulations in relation to full-size medals differ from those for the other services (as detailed in Section 7), in the following particulars:

(a) In the case of Ratings and ranks below officer, medals should overlap whenever *three* or more are worn. The length of bar in respect of these personnel is 95mm (3¾ ins.) for three medals, and up to a maximum of 171mm (6¾ ins.) for larger numbers.

(b) The length of riband for medals of normal size is 44mm (1¾ ins.) measuring from the top of the riband to the ring or suspension bar. A 44mm riband will accommodate four clasps, but if more than four are worn the length of the riband should be adjusted to allow 13mm (½in.) to be visible above the topmost clasp. The length of riband on adjacent medals may also need to be adjusted in order to ensure that the medals are in line at their lowest points.

4. Medal Ribbons
● Medal ribbons only are worn with *No. 1C Dress* and *No. 1CW Dress (Warm Weather)*.
    When worn by Royal Navy personnel ribbons are 13mm (½ in.) in depth, i.e. from

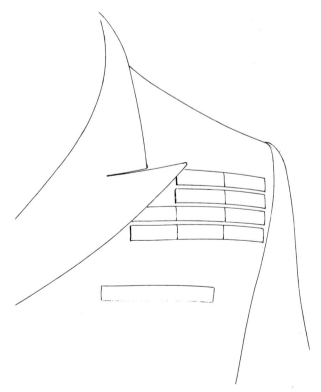

Royal Navy – Arrangement of medal ribbons, No. 1C Dress.

the top to bottom edge, but when five or more rows are worn the ribbon is 10mm ($\frac{3}{8}$ in.) deep. With *No. 1C Dress* the ribbons are sewn on the garments, but with *No. 1CW Dress* a detachable, brooch-type ribbon bar is worn with the pin inserted through beckets in the correct positions.

Officers. Each row of ribbons should be 6mm ($\frac{1}{4}$ in.) apart, but officers may reduce this distance in order to accommodate a large number of rows. The ribbons in each row should all be visible and not covered by the left lapel. The top or only row should be 25mm (1 in.) below the point of the shoulder. The layout of ribbons will be governed largely by the uniform's lapel, and will mean that the topmost row or rows will contain fewer ribbons than any that follow below, but the overall arrangement should be kept as symmetrical as possible. The detachable bar (usually worn with warm-weather tunics and bush-jackets), may also have more than one row, as necessary, and no row should be longer than the one immediately above.

Ratings. On Senior Ratings' jackets, the top, or only row of ribbons should be positioned on a level with the point of the left lapel. With Junior Ratings' blue (or white) jumpers, it should be 114mm ($4\frac{1}{2}$ ins.) below the point of the shoulder. On white uniform it should be 51mm (2 ins.) below the point of the shoulder. No row is to be shorter than the one above, and the arrangement should be as symmetrical as possible. A gap of 3mm ($\frac{1}{8}$ in.) should intervene between each row.

The Royal Marines

The uniforms of the Royal Marines on which orders, decorations and medals are worn are the **Full Ceremonial Dress**, the **No. 1A Blue Dress**, and the **No. 1B Lovat Dress** (the latter two being of Corps 'open neck' pattern).

● *Full Ceremonial Dress.* General Officers wearing the 'high neck' *Full Ceremonial Dress* are entitled to wear, besides their full-size decorations and medals, a broad riband (or Collar when specially ordered), up to four breast stars, and up to three neck-badges (two on Joint Service occasions). The medal-bar should be positioned on the left side on a level just below the top button of the tunic. A single breast star should be situated centrally below it, equidistant between the lower edges of the medals and the sash belt. Two stars should be arranged so that the senior is centred just below the medals, and the second is aligned immediately below it. Three stars should be arranged in a triangular formation, and four in a diamond formation. The senior or only neck-badge is suspended from a short length of riband emerging at the bottom of the collar beneath the hook and eye. A second neck-badge is suspended below it from a 76mm (3 ins.) length of riband attached by hook and eye to the inside of the tunic.

● *No. 1A Blue Dress and No. 1B Lovat Dress.* These orders of dress are worn on 'full ceremonial' and 'ceremonial' occasions. Single decorations and medals, or mounted groups of full-size medals, are worn centrally above the left breast pocket, the lower edges of the medals just above the pocket button (the medals should cover any ribbons). Up to three neck-badges may be worn on 'full ceremonial' occasions (two on Joint Service occasions), and one only on 'ceremonial' occasions. An officer wears his senior or only neck-badge suspended from a miniature width riband worn under the shirt collar, with the top of the suspension ring immediately below the knot of the tie. A second badge is suspended 19mm (3¼ in.) below the top button of the jacket from a riband attached to an eye stitched inside the tunic. Up to two breast stars may be worn with these uniforms; a single star should be situated centrally on the breast pocket below the medal-bar. When two stars are worn, the senior should be positioned with its topmost point just below, or just touching, the lip of the breast pocket, the second star being aligned immediately below it.

● *Medal ribbons*: Medal ribbons only are worn with *No. 1C Dress*. All ribbons are 10mm (⅜ in.) in depth, i.e. from top to bottom edge. The first row is worn centrally over the left breast pocket, 6mm (¼ in.) above the top seam of the pocket. Additional rows are placed centrally over the first with no row shorter than the one above. A distance of 6mm (¼ in.) should intervene between each row. There should be no more than five ribbons to a row, and no row must extend nearer than 20mm (¾ in.) from the shoulder seam. Each row must be completed before another is started.

The Army

1. Full Dress, No. 1 Dress (Ceremonial), and No. 3 Dress (Warm Weather)
are 'high neck' uniforms which are worn on **'full ceremonial day'** occasions.
Orders, decorations and medals are worn with them as follows:

(a) The Collar and/or Broad Riband and Badge are worn as described above on pp. 73–74.

(b) Breast Stars
Full Dress
Up to four stars may be worn, and are displayed in the same formations as are given
immediately below for *No. 1* and *No. 3 Dress* and in corresponding positions.

No. 1 Dress (Ceremonial) and No. 3 Dress (Ceremonial, Warm Weather)
Up to four stars may be worn, their positions as follows:
   One star: centre of the breast pocket, the upper point not less than 25mm (1 in.)
below the lip of the pocket.
   Two stars: one above the other, the senior centrally in line below the pocket
button so that its topmost point is just below, or just touching the lip of the pocket;
the second star aligned below the first, its topmost point not less than 25mm below
the lowest point of the first star.
   Three stars: a triangular formation with the senior star at the top, its topmost
point directly below the pocket button, the other two stars being placed either side of
it, below; the second star is worn nearest the centre of the chest. If this arrangement
interferes with a broad riband passing from right shoulder to left hip, two options are
possible: (i) Army officers are permitted to invert the triangular arrangement of stars
so that the first and second are worn side by side below the medal-bar, with the first
positioned towards the centre of the chest, and the third centrally below; or (ii) the
bow of the riband can be brought forward a little to rest on the front of the hip,
thereby allowing more space on the lower left side for the stars.
   Four stars: a diamond formation, the first three stars being positioned in
triangular fashion, with the fourth placed centrally below the second and third stars
in vertical line with the first.

● Note: if two, three or four stars are to be worn, the medal-bar must be placed at a
sufficiently high point on the left side of the uniform to allow the stars to be attached
below it so that they avoid touching the waist sash or belt.

(c) Neck Decorations
A maximum of three neck-badges may be worn with these uniforms (two on 'Joint
Service' occasions). They must be displayed in descending order of seniority,
beginning with Knight Commanders' badges, then those of Companion and/or
Commander.

The *senior* badge is worn on a miniature width riband around the neck inside the collar of the jacket or tunic, and hangs from the bottom of the collar on about 20mm (¾ in.) of riband. (Alternatively, a riband slip, with the badge suspended, is attached to the inside front of the collar by means of a hook and eye.) The *second* badge, if one is worn, is suspended from a riband slip, of which about 20mm should be visible, attached by hook and eye to the inside of the tunic; the riband slip should be attached so that a space of about 25mm (1 in.) intervenes between the bottom of the first badge and top of the second. A *third* neck-badge should be suspended and positioned in a similar fashion below the second.

(d) Single Medals/Medal Brooch-Bar

A mounted group of full-size medals, or a single full-size medal or decoration, should be worn on the left side of the uniform coat. The medals are situated on the left side at a level approximately midway between the first and second buttons from the bottom of the collar. In the case of *No. 1 Dress* and *No. 3 Dress,* the beckets should be situated so that the medals cover as best as possible any medal ribbons stitched to the garment. It may be necessary, however, to position the medals at a somewhat higher point if it is intended to wear two or more breast stars.

● *Court Mounted Medals.* The back of the frame should be covered by a black face cloth or doeskin, with the exception of the Guards Division, whose medals are backed with scarlet.

2. The Frock Coat

General Officers. This is a double-breasted coat, and is worn mainly on ceremonial occasions, but may also be worn on some non-ceremonial occasions (such as Investitures) with ribbons only. The *medal-bar* should be positioned just below the top left-hand button (beckets should be situated so that the medal-bar covers any medal ribbons sewn to the coat). Up to four *breast stars* may be worn on 'full ceremonial' occasions, and two on 'ceremonial' occasions. A single star should be worn midway between the bottom edges of the medals and the waist sash, and to the left of the uniform's left-hand row of buttons. With two stars, the senior should be positioned a little higher allowing the second to be aligned beneath it. Three stars are arranged in a triangular formation, with the second and third stars (in this precedence) placed either side below the first. It may prove necessary for the second star to cover one or more of the left hand row of buttons. A fourth star is worn centrally below, in vertical line with the first. A *broad riband* passing from the right shoulder will need to be worn so that the bow and badge rest on the front of the left hip ensuring sufficient space for the second and fourth stars, and that they are not unduly obscured.

One *neck-badge* only is permissible at Single Service events; it is suspended from a miniature-width riband, of which about 20mm (¾ in.) should be visible, and is connected by hook and eye to the inside of the collar. At Joint Service events two neck decorations may be worn, the second badge being suspended from the collar by a longer length of miniature- width riband which hangs behind the first badge.

Army – General's Frock Coat.   The collar and badge appendant of the senior Order is worn (in this case GCB), with the broad riband and badge of the next senior Order (in this case GCVO).   Three breast stars (GCB, GCVO and Bailiff Grand Cross, Order of St. John), and one neck decoration are worn (in this case CBE).   The medal-bar commences with the MC and is followed by campaign and other medals.

Household Division Officers.   The frock coats worn by both Household Cavalry and Foot Guards are single-breasted and trimmed with loops of black braid. This is traditionally an Undress uniform and is never worn with medals.   Medal ribbons are worn between the first and second loops of braid.   One breast star may be worn (plus one of a foreign order if appropriate) on suitable occasions.   The only neck-badges permitted with this type of frock coat are those of the *Order of Merit* and the *Order of the Companions of Honour.* Broad ribands are not worn.

3. No. 1 Dress, No. 3 Dress (Warm Weather), No. 2 Dress (Service Dress), and No. 4 Dress (Warm Weather Service Dress)

The *No. 1* and *No. 3 Dress* have 'high' collars, and *No. 2* and *No. 4 Dress* are 'open neck' uniforms. On **'ceremonial day'** occasions orders, decorations and medals are worn in the following manner with these uniforms:

(a) Breast Stars

A maximum of two stars may be worn. *One star* is positioned in the centre of the left breast pocket, the upper point not less than 25mm (1 in.) below the lip of the breast pocket. With *two stars* the senior star is placed with its topmost point just below, or just touching the lip of the breast pocket, centrally in line below the pocket button. The second star should be aligned below, its topmost point not less than 25mm below the lowest point of the first star.

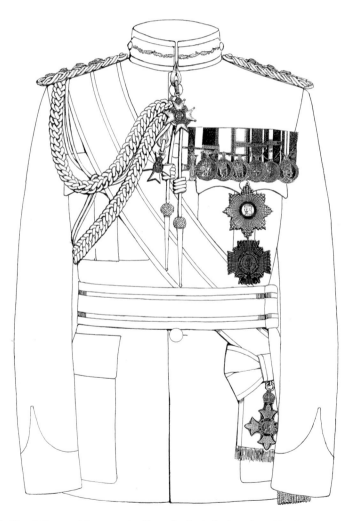

Army – General's No. 1 Dress (Ceremonial). The broad riband and badge of the senior award (in this case GBE) is worn, with two breast stars (GBE and KCB), and two neck decorations (of KCB and CVO). The medal-bar commences with the MC and is followed by campaign and other medals.

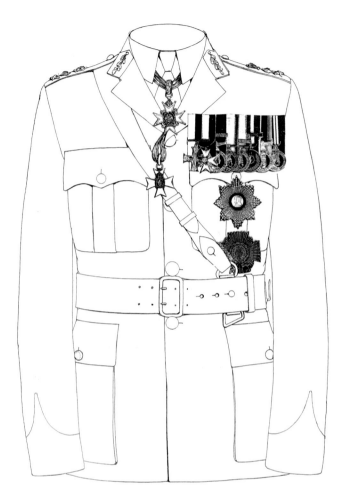

Army – General's No. 2 Dress (Service Dress). This shows the maximum of insignia which may be worn with Service Dress, two breast stars (in this case GBE and KCB), and two neck decorations (of KCB and CVO). The medal-bar commences with the breast decorations of MC and Officer, Order of St. John and is followed by campaign and other medals.

(b) Neck Decorations

One neck decoration only may be worn on 'ceremonial' occasions. However, this restriction is increased to two when there is a need for these uniforms to be worn on 'full ceremonial' occasions. With *No. 1 Dress* and *No. 3 Dress*, badges are worn as described above for 'full ceremonial' occasions.

In respect of *No. 2 Dress* and *No. 4 Dress*, the Army's 'Materiel Regulations' state that badges must be suspended from ribands of Companion or Membership width. It is now customary, however, for senior officers to wear their badges suspended from miniature-width ribands. The riband of the *senior*, or only badge is worn around the neck and under the shirt collar, with the top of the badge's suspension ring at 20mm (¾ in.) below the knot of the tie. A *second* badge may be worn below the first, suspended from a riband slip, attached by hook and eye to the inside of the tunic just above the top buttonhole, of which about 20mm should be visible.

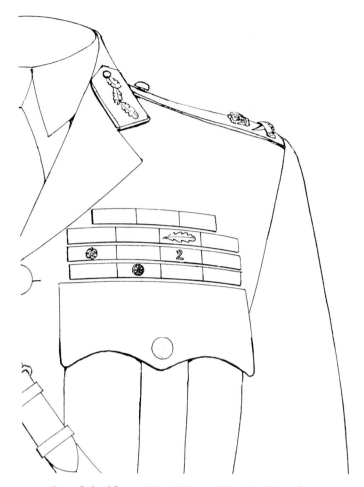

Army – Arrangement of medal ribbons, No. 2 Dress (Service Dress).

Chaplains in *No. 2* and *No. 4 Dress* wear the neck-badge riband over the clerical stock.

(c) Single Medals/Medal Brooch-Bar
A single full-size medal or decoration, or mounted group of full-size decorations and medals, should be worn on the left side of the tunic or jacket. The medal-bar should be accommodated by beckets situated above the top row of ribbons which should not be visible when the medals themselves are worn. It may be necessary, however, to position the medals at a somewhat higher point if it is intended to wear two breast stars.

4.   No. 6 Dress (with Sam Browne belt)
When this uniform is worn on **'full ceremonial day'** or **'ceremonial day'** occasions, only single full-size breast decorations or medals, or a mounted group of full-size decorations and medals, should be worn. No other insignia are permitted with this uniform.

5. Medal Ribbons

● Medal Ribbons alone are worn on **non-ceremonial occasions** with the *Nos. 1, 2, 3, 4,* and *6 Dress* and the *Frock Coat (General Officers' and Household Division Officers)*.

When worn by Army personnel, ribbons are 9.5mm (⅜ in.) in depth, i.e. from the top to bottom edge. They should be worn above the left breast pocket *(Nos. 1, 2, 3, 4,* and *6 Dress)*. A single ribbon, or incomplete row of ribbons, should be centred over the breast pocket button. The maximum number of ribbons in each row is either four or five, depending on the physique of the individual and the type of uniform coat, i.e. whether it has a high collar or open neck. As many ribbons as possible should be placed in a row before another is started, but they should be positioned so that none is totally hidden by a lapel. When two or more rows are worn and there are insufficient ribbons to complete a row, it is the top row which is incomplete, starting with the ribbons of an individual's most senior orders, decorations or medals, and should be placed centrally above the topmost *complete* row. In each *complete* row, the outer edges of the ribbons closest to the shoulder must be vertically in line with that in the bottom row. Where ribbons are worn in two or more rows, individuals must comply with these general principles, but may use their discretion in deciding the number of ribbons to be placed in each row. Rows are to be approximately 3mm (⅛ in.) apart, but if more than four rows are worn, they should not be spaced.

General Officers' Frock Coat. Ribbons should be positioned so that the lower or only row of ribbons is centred on the left side, immediately above the second button from the collar in the left-hand row. Their layout follows the same principles as for other uniforms above.

Household Division Officers' Frock Coat. Ribbons are worn between the first and second loops of braid, and observe the same principles of layout as for other uniforms above.

Warm weather garments. Ribbons may not be stitched directly on to warm weather garments, but should be worn on detachable 'step' brooches.

6. Regimental and other Military Uniforms

There are other uniforms on which orders, decorations and medals are worn which have not been highlighted in this Section. These include the uniforms of individual Army regiments, the Directors of Music and bandsmen, as well as ceremonial units such as the Military Knights of Windsor, the Honourable Corps of Gentlemen-at-Arms, and the Yeomen of the Guard. Although all but the latter of these uniforms approximate to the types of 'military' pattern which have been covered in this Section, the presence of accoutrements may necessitate slight adjustments or allowances in the manner in which some insignia and medals are worn. The general principle, for example, that medals should be entirely visible, may not always be possible with some uniforms. The commonest obstacles are the cross-belts worn with some regimental uniforms across the body from left shoulder and under the right arm, which may need to cover the top right hand corner of a mounted group of medals. Exceptions to this practice are seen in Scotland where members of the Royal Company of Archers wear the medal-bar over the cross-belt. Similarly, the pipers of

Scottish Regiments wear medals on the cross-plaid worn over the left shoulder. The positioning of neck decorations (when two or more are worn) may also require a degree of improvisation. Cross-belts on other uniforms, whether worn over right or left shoulders, are always worn *over* any broad ribands of the Orders of Knighthood.

The Royal Air Force

1.   No. 1 Dress, No. 1A Dress and No. 6 Dress (Men and Women)

On **'full ceremonial day'** occasions, orders, medals and decorations are worn with these uniforms in the following manner:

(a) The Collar and/or Broad Riband and Badge are worn as described above on pp. 73–74.

(b) Breast Stars

Royal Air Force officers may normally wear a maximum of three stars with these uniforms at any one time, and up to four if one of them is the star of a foreign order.

One star: centre of the breast pocket, the upper point being not less than 25mm (1 in.) below the lip of the pocket.

Two stars: one above the other, the senior star centred below the pocket button, its topmost point just below, or just touching the lip of the breast pocket, and the second star aligned directly below it.

Three stars: a triangular formation with the senior star at the top, centrally below the pocket button, the other two stars (in second and third order of precedence) in a lower position on either side of it. Should this arrangement interfere with with a broad riband that passes from right shoulder to left hip, the bow of the riband can be brought forward a little to rest on the front of the hip, which will allow more space for the stars.

Four stars: a diamond formation, the first three stars positioned according to precedence as above, with the fourth centrally below stars two and three, and in vertical line with the first.

● Note: if two, three or four stars are to be worn, the medal-bar must be placed at a sufficiently high point on the left side of the uniform to allow the stars to be attached below without their encroaching on the waist sash or belt.

(c) Neck Decorations

A maximum of two neck decorations (including one foreign neck decoration) may be worn with these uniforms, and should appear in descending seniority. The riband of the *senior* or only badge is worn around the neck and under the shirt collar, with the top of the badge's suspension ring at 20mm (¾ in.) below the knot of the tie. A *second* badge may be worn below the first, suspended from a riband slip, attached by hook and eye to the inside of the tunic at the top buttonhole, of which about 20mm should be visible. Chaplains wear the neck-badge riband over the clerical stock.

● *No. 6 Dress (Women).* When wearing this warm weather dress style uniform, women wear their senior, or only neck decoration on a bow fashioned from the full-size riband of the appropriate order. The bow is worn on the left side of the dress, centrally below the full-size medal brooch-bar; any breast star or stars are centred directly below the bow.

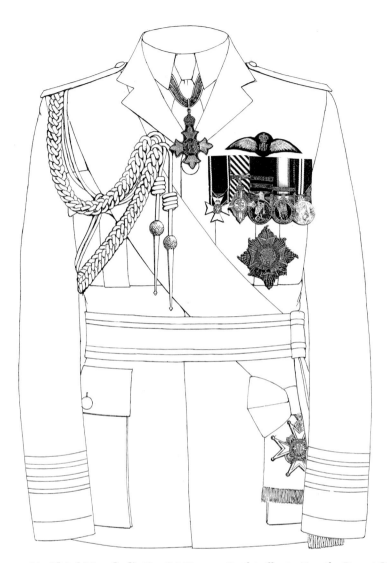

Royal Air Force – Air Chief Marshal's No. 1A Dress. In this illustration the Breast Star, Broad Riband and Badge of GCB is worn, together with the neck decoration of CBE. The medal-bar commences with the breast decorations of LVO and the AFC and is followed by campaign and other medals.

(d) Single Medals/Medal Brooch-Bar

A single full-size medal or decoration, or mounted group of full-size medals, should be worn on the left side of the uniform coat. Medals may be mounted 'court style' or 'ordinary style'. The medal-bar is attached by means of beckets sewn to the uniform above the top row of medal ribbons stitched to the jacket so that these are not visible when the medals themselves are worn. It may be necessary to position the medal-bar at a somewhat higher point if it is intended to wear two or more breast stars.

Royal Air Force – Arrangement of medal ribbons, No. 1 Dress.

On **'ceremonial day'** occasions, with the *No. 1, No. 1A, No. 6* and *No. 6A Dress* uniforms, mounted groups of full-size medals, or single decorations and medals are worn. The may be accompanied by a maximum of **two** breast stars (one of which may be of a foreign order) and **one** neck decoration. These insignia are positioned in the manner described above for 'full ceremonial day' occasions. No other insignia may be worn.

When No. 6B Parade Dress (warm weather areas) is worn on **'ceremonial day'** occasions, only mounted groups of full-size decorations and medals, or single decorations and medals, and no other insignia, may be worn. The medals are centred on the left side, using the same beckets as would be used for a detachable ribbon bar.

2. **Medal Ribbons**

● Medal Ribbons alone are worn on **non-ceremonial occasions** with *No. 1, 6, 6B, 10* and *11 Dress.*

When worn by Royal Air Force personnel ribbons are 11mm. ($\frac{7}{16}$ in.) in depth, i.e. from the top to bottom edge. The bottom or only row should be located immediately and centrally above the flap of the left breast pocket (or in the corresponding position where a pocket is not fitted). The senior ribbon is worn nearest the lapel, and in the top row when more than one row is worn.   A row should not consist of more than four ribbons, but when more than four are worn, they should be arranged to display as many complete rows of four as possible, with any *incomplete* row being placed centrally at the top and containing the ribbons of the most senior awards held. Beginning with the bottom row, each succeeding row should be placed centrally above the preceding one.   When the ribbons of any row or rows are likely to be wholly or partly obscured by the lapel or collar of the jacket, the row is shortened to display completely as many ribbons as possible in the space between the edge of the lapel/collar and the sleeve-head seam.   The edges of the ribbons nearest the shoulder in each *complete* row of four (or each shortened row) should be vertically in line with the far edge of the bottom row.   A space of 3mm ($\frac{1}{8}$ in.) should intervene between each row, but if four or more rows are worn, they should not be spaced.

With warm-weather dress (*Nos. 6, 6B* and *11 Dresses*), ribbons should be mounted on detachable brooches.

Mess Dress

There is little variation in the regulations for the wearing of orders, decorations and medals with Mess Dress for each of the Services, and the similarity between the uniform styles obviates any need to explain separately the rules obtaining in each case.   In the notes that follow, slight differences where they occur for one or other of the main Services, or specific directions in relation to particular insignia have, of course, been indicated and explained where necessary.   The rules concerning miniature badges, orders, decorations and medals are given in full in Section 7.

● The Collars of the Orders of Knighthood are **not** at any time worn with Mess Dress or Evening Uniform

(a) The Broad (Sash) Riband
The broad riband of an Order of Knighthood is only worn on **'full ceremonial evening'** occasions.
   It is worn under the jacket but over the waistcoat (or cummerbund).   With evening wear the riband is a shortened version of the full-length riband and does not pass over the shoulder and down the back of the body as it would if worn with full uniform. The shortened riband should be tailored to fit the body correctly and the top edge fashioned to avoid sagging. The riband has two buttonholes at the far end of the longer, 'display' section which are fastened to two buttons situated at the front of the armhole of the waistcoat.   The riband passes diagonally across the front of the waistcoat, and the other, short end of the riband, shaped into a point and having a buttonhole, fastens to a button situated at the lower side of waistcoat.   This enables the bow and badge to rest on the right or left hip where it should be clearly visible.
   With Mess Dress uniforms which do not include a waistcoat, the display section of the riband is attached in the same positions to the shirt and cummerbund.

(b) Breast Stars
Up to four stars may be worn by men and women on **'full ceremonial evening'** occasions, and up to two on **'ceremonial evening'** occasions.   They are worn in the same formations as with uniform, and with the numerical restrictions applicable to each of the Services. Stars are attached by means of beckets sewn on to the mess jacket.   On appropriate occasions the star of a foreign order may be worn.

● *Royal Air Force*.   The RAF lays down specific regulations regarding the location of individual stars in relation to the jacket buttons:
   One star: centrally, covering the middle button.
   Two stars: one above the other, the senior between the top and middle buttons, and the second between the middle and bottom buttons.
   Three stars: a triangular formation, with the senior at the apex between the top and middle buttons, and the other two (in second and third order of precedence) horizontally in line between the middle and bottom buttons.
   Four stars: a diamond formation, the topmost star between the top and middle

Mess Dress – Royal Navy, Admiral.   The broad riband and badge of the senior Order is worn (in this case GCB), with three breast stars (GCB, KBE and Knight of Justice, Order of St. John), and the senior neck decoration (of KBE). These three awards, together with the breast decorations of LVO and DSC, are represented in their correct sequence on the miniature brooch-bar.

buttons; the two central stars worn horizontally in line between the middle and bottom buttons; and the lower star vertically in line with the top one.

(c) Neck Decoration

One neck decoration only may be worn on either **'full ceremonial evening'** or **'ceremonial evening'** occasions. It should be the senior to which the wearer is entitled. On appropriate occasions the neck decoration of a foreign order may be worn.

The full-size badge is suspended from a miniature width riband (16mm or ⅝ in.), and is fastened at the back with a 'hook and eye'. The riband should fit neatly around the lower edge of the collar of the shirt (emerging at either side from under the neck band of the white or black tie) and below the collar 'wings' and the bow tie, so that

Mess Dress – Army, General.   The broad riband and badge of the senior Order is worn (in the case GCB), with the maximum of four breast stars (in this case GCB, GCVO, KBE and Knight of Justice, Order of St. John), and the senior neck decoration (of KBE). These four awards, together with the MC, are represented in correct sequence on the miniature brooch-bar.

---

the badge hangs centrally with the top of the suspension ring no more than 25mm below the tie knot. If a soft 'turn down' collar is worn, the riband is worn under the collar.

(d) Miniature Decorations and Medals

Single miniatures or groups of miniature orders, decorations and medals are worn on **'full ceremonial evening'** and **'ceremonial evening'** occasions. When worn with Mess Dress on **'non-ceremonial evening'** occasions, miniatures are worn on their own with no other insignia.

   The miniature brooch-bar is worn on the left lapel of the Mess Dress/Undress jacket. If need be, a longer brooch may extend leftwards on to the shoulder area of the coat and be partly attached there. However, the bar must not extend beyond the shoulder seam, nor beyond the inner edge of the left lapel.

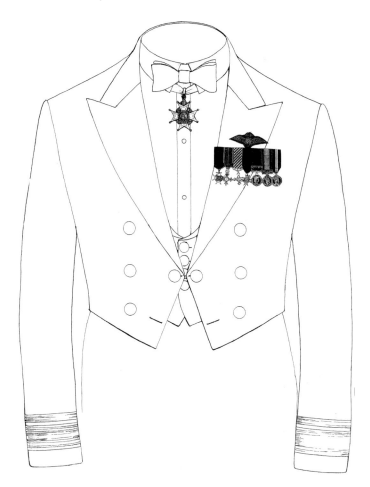

Mess Dress – Royal Air Force, Air Vice-Marshal. The neck decoration of CB is worn, and together with the breast decorations of OBE, DFC and Officer, Order of St. John, is represented on the miniature brooch-bar.

● *Royal Marines.* By colonels and ranks above, the miniature brooch-bar is worn on the lapel 102mm (4 ins.) below the neck point of the shoulder seam. By other officers it is worn 19mm (¾ in.) below the RM globe and laurel badge.

● *Royal Air Force.* The brooch-bar is worn on the lapel 13mm (½ in.) below a flying badge, or the same distance below a medical, dental, or chaplaincy collar ensign, or in a corresponding position when there is no entitlement to a badge.

(e) Miniature ribbon-bar

Miniature ribbon bars may only be worn with Mess Dress, and are currently only worn by officers of the Royal Navy when acting as Duty Officers. Miniature ribbons are 10mm (⅜ in.) in depth, i.e. from the top to bottom edge, and 19mm (¾ in.) wide. They are not sewn to the garment but are worn on detachable brooch-type bars in the same position as miniature medals.

11. Robes, Court Dress, Civil and Ceremonial Uniform

Peers' and Peeresses' Parliamentary Robes

On those occasions in the House of Lords when peers and peeresses are required to wear parliamentary robes, collars should be worn by those who are Knights or Ladies Companion of the Garter, or Knights or Ladies of the Thistle, or who are Knights or Dames Grand Cross of the other Orders of Knighthood. Peers and peeresses wear the collar of the most senior Order they hold. The collar, with its appendant badge, is placed over the shoulders, as near as possible to the extreme point of each shoulder, and should hang down equally at both the front and back of the robe, with the badge

Peer's Parliamentary Robe. The collar (in this case GCMG) as worn by a Life Peer (Baron) in Parliamentary Robes. The collar is attached to each shoulder by means of satin bows.

suspended below front centre. The collar is fastened at the shoulders by white satin bows, the material for which is 38mm (1½ ins.) wide. No other insignia are worn. This latter requirement also applies if a Service or ceremonial uniform is worn under the robe.

Judges' Robes

The Judges' 'Guide to Robing' prescribes the wearing of 'decorations' with full ceremonial robes on certain ceremonial occasions during the course of the legal year. These include the procession to, and service at Westminster Abbey to mark the opening of the legal year at the beginning of the Michaelmas sittings in October; the presentation of the incoming Lord Mayor of London to the Lord Chief Justice and other members of the judiciary (Lord Mayor's Day); in the presence of the Sovereign in the House of Lords (State Opening of Parliament); the Guildhall Banquet and other official events at the Guildhall and elsewhere which are designated 'white tie' occasions; Sunday cathedral services; and at the swearing-in of judges by the Lord Chancellor and by the Lord Chief Justice.

On such occasions, and at other times when specified, senior members of the judiciary who wear the black silk and gold lace gown (namely, the Lord Chancellor, the Master of the Rolls, the Vice-Chancellor, the Lord Justices of Appeal, and the Presidents of the Probate, Divorce, Admiralty and Family Divisions), do not normally wear insignia of any kind, save for when the incumbent is a lady in which case the insignia of DBE is worn on the upper left-hand side of the court coat. Gentlemen who are Puisne (or High Court) Judges, on these occasions habited in their scarlet and ermine robes, may wear a mounted group of full-size decorations and medals (or a single full-size decoration or medal), on the upper left side of their scarlet and ermine-trimmed hoods, but it is not usual for them to wear any other items of insignia. Ladies who are High Court Judges wear their DBE insignia, the bow decoration on the upper left side of the hood and the star centred below it. Beckets for the purposes of attaching insignia to the hood should be correctly situated and sewn in to place.

Circuit Judges, when attending an event where 'decorations' are specified, may also wear full-size medals on the left side of their violet-coloured hoods, but other insignia are not usually worn.

Queen's Counsels' Robes

At their swearing-in and on specified ceremonial occasions Queen's Counsel, attired in their full ceremonial robes, may wear a mounted group of full-size decorations and medals (or a single full-size decoration or medal). The medals are worn on the upper area of the left front panel of their black silk gowns, and are attached by means of beckets sewn into place. Other insignia are not usually worn.

Court Dress

Full Court Dress consists of a black 'court coat' (velvet or black cloth), waistcoat, knee breeches and stockings, buckled shoes, lace jabot and cuffs, and a silver-hilted dress sword. This outfit is worn by gentlemen on some ceremonial occasions, by High Sheriffs, and by certain officials at the Palace of Westminster such as the Gentleman Usher of the Black Rod, the Serjeant-at-Arms, the Clerk of the Parliaments, and the Clerk of the House of Commons. The usual occasion on which the latter officials wear insignia with Court Dress is at the State Opening of Parliament.

The wearing of insignia with Court Dress follows broadly the same format as for Morning Dress, the major difference being that mounted decorations and medals (or a single decoration or medal) are worn in miniature. The miniatures should be worn in the customary position on the upper left side of the coat, but positioned so that they are obscured as little as possible by the lace jabot. Stars may be worn below the medals up to the number of four and in the usual formations described elsewhere. A single neck-badge may be worn; this is suspended from a miniature-width riband which should fit around the lower edge of the jabot stock; the badge itself should hang centrally and rest on the upper part of the jabot. The collar of an Order of Knighthood may be worn; it should hang at an equal distance back and front, and be attached at the shoulders with white satin bows. Black Rod wears, in addition, his chain and badge of office, and the Serjeant-at-Arms wears an official Collar of SS.

Ceremonial Uniform

Various other kinds of ceremonial uniform or dress are worn on ceremonial or state occasions. The wearing of insignia with these uniforms follows the same format as for Service uniforms. Full-size mounted decorations and medals (or a single decoration or medal) are worn on the upper left side, beneath which up to four stars may be worn according to the designated formations; up to three neck-badges may be worn; a broad riband may be worn, which must be the senior to which the wearer is entitled. The collar of an Order of Knighthood should be worn when specially ordered, in which case the broad riband of the same Order may not be worn.

● *Great Officers of State.* These are principally the red and gold-embroidered coatee uniforms of the Earl Marshal and the Lord Great Chamberlain, and the red and gold tunic of the Master of the Horse. When the Collar of an Order of Knighthood is worn, it is attached to the shoulders with white satin bows.

● *Lord-Lieutenants.* The full dress uniform of a Lord-Lieutenant equates with that of the Army's No 1 Dress (Ceremonial) for the rank of major-general. Lord-Lieutenants who are entitled to wear the Baronet's Badge should bear in mind that it precedes all other neck-badges in the 'order of wear' except the OM, and that it should therefore be accorded this precedence when worn.

• *Colonial governors.* In warm-weather climates governors wear the white tunic uniform; in temperate zones they wear the traditional dark blue double-breasted coatee with aiguilettes.

Uniformed Public Services

When in full uniform, members of the Police Services wear the ribbon strips in respect of decorations and medals which they have been awarded; these are centred immediately above the left breast pocket. On ceremonial occasions a group of mounted decorations and medals (or a single decoration or medal) must be positioned on the uniform so as to cover those ribbons that are stitched to the tunic. Senior police officers who are Knight Bachelors may at their option wear either the Knight Bachelor's Neck-Badge or Breast-Badge, or both; the Knight Bachelor's Neck-Badge takes precedence over all Third Class (Companion or Commander) badges of the Orders of Knighthood, and should be worn accordingly. No more than two neck decorations may be worn. (See p. 85 for the correct method of wearing neck-badges with 'open neck' style uniform).

Women in full uniform are required on ceremonial occasions to wear as a neck decoration any bow decoration they may hold of Third Class (Companion or Commander), or higher. (For further details see p. 34). A woman who is a chief constable and is a DBE will therefore wear as a neck-badge her converted bow decoration, plus the star centrally below her brooch-bar containing other full-size decorations and medals.

These practices are also observed by serving members of other public services such as the Fire Services, and organisations such as the Order of St. John, when wearing their 'open neck' uniforms. Undress ribbons of decorations and medals are worn on these uniforms in the usual fashion immediately above the breast pocket, but when specially required decorations and medals and other insignia are worn in the manner described above.

Municipal Robes

Orders, decorations and medals are not usually worn with municipal robes on the practical grounds that they would not be seen on morning dress or lounge suits worn under aldermanic and similar such gowns. Insignia are not to be worn on the gowns themselves. An exception to these strictures relates to the neck-badges of Orders which on ceremonial occasions are worn with robes by members of the Corporation of the City of London. One badge only is worn and is suspended from a miniature-width riband. If a lace jabot is worn, the riband should fit around the lower edge of the neck stock.

Clerical Robes

At special religious services, particularly those attended by The Queen or other Members of the Royal Family, or services in remembrance of military events, insignia may be worn by the officiating clergymen. Decorations and medals mounted in a group (or a single decoration or medal) are worn on the black tippet or 'preaching scarf' worn stole-wise over the white surplice (and by archbishops and bishops over the red outer robe or chimere). Beckets or eyelets should be correctly situated on the tippet to accommodate the medals on the upper left hand side. The star of an Order of Knighthood, or the Order of St. John, is also worn on the tippet and below any medals. The neck-badge of an Order may be worn suspended from a miniature-width riband which should fit around the clerical stock; the badge should hang so that the top of its suspension ring is no more than 38mm (1½ ins.) below the stock.

On all other occasions the undress ribbons of decorations and medals may as a matter of personal choice be worn on a brooch attached to the tippet (and using the same beckets).

It is not usual to wear medals or the star of an Order when ornamental vestments are worn, although neck-badges can be worn.

Where it is required or necessary, a mounted group of medals (or a single decoration or medal) may be worn on the cassock. Beckets for this purpose should be tailored to the correct position on the upper left hand side.

Academic Robes

It is not usual for orders, decorations and medals to be worn with full academic dress unless this is expressly permitted under the statutes of the university concerned. If worn at all, insignia should be worn under the gown, but wearers should bear in mind that with lounge suit it is appropriate to wear only a medal-bar (or a single decoration or medal) and one neck-badge or bow decoration. (See pp. 59–61, 70–71).

12. Services for the Orders of Knighthood

Services of dedication and remembrance are held at intervals for each of the Orders of Knighthood at their respective churches or chapels. These are important ceremonial events, and are usually attended by The Queen, who is Sovereign of each of the Orders, or other Members of the Royal Family. Announcements of these occasions are made in *The Times* and *The Daily Telegraph* or by personal notification well in advance, and arrangements, including those in respect of invitations to guests, are made by the Central Chancery of the Orders of Knighthood. (In the case of the Order of the British Empire, the extensive membership of the Order and limited seating capacity in St. Paul's Cathedral prohibits the issue of tickets to spouses or guests who are not members or medallists of the Order). All members of an Order who attend a service are required to wear their insignia in accordance with the following directions:

● **Garter and Thistle Services.**
At a service of the Order of the Garter (St. George's Chapel, Windsor), or of the Order of the Thistle (St. Giles' Cathedral, Edinburgh), Knights wear morning dress with their star attached to the left side of the coat. Medals and other insignia are not worn. The mantle is worn over the morning dress coat. The collar is worn over the mantle, being attached to the shoulders with white satin bows, and should hang at an equal distance back and front, with the collar badge at the front. Ladies of these Orders wear their mantles over a long dress, on the left side of which they wear the star.

● **Other Orders of Knighthood.**
Knights and Dames Grand Cross wear the mantle of the Order which is tied at the front with tasselled cords. The collar is hung over the shoulders, where it is attached with white satin bows, and should hang at an equal distance back and front, with the badge at the front. (Where necessary, mantles are supplied for these occasions by the Central Chancery). At a service for the Order of the Bath (Westminster Abbey), the Order of St. Michael and St. George (St. Paul's Cathedral), or the Order of the British Empire (St. Paul's Cathedral), Knights and Dames Grand Cross do not need to wear their star as this is represented by the embroidered version on their mantles. The star is, however, worn by GCVOs at the Order's services at St. George's Chapel, Windsor, since a reception is normally held immediately afterwards at which insignia are worn.

Other Classes and Medallists: Members of the other classes of the Orders, and those who are holders of the Royal Victorian Medal and the British Empire Medal, wear *only* the insignia of the Order for which the service is being held. This will mean, for example, that if a gentleman or lady who is a KBE/DBE and a CB attends a service for the Order of the Bath at Westminster Abbey, he or she will wear only the CB Badge as a neck or bow decoration. A Knight or Dame Commander of an Order for which a service is being held will wear only the star of the Order, and *not* the associate neck-badge. (*Note*: Since gentlemen have the option of wearing insignia on these occasions with either Morning Dress or Lounge Suit, they are permitted to wear the breast star of a Knight Commander on a suit jacket. This is, however, the only circumstance in which a breast star may be worn with lounge suit.)

At a service for the Royal Victorian Order or for the Order of the British Empire, a gentleman or lady who is an LVO, MVO, OBE, or MBE, or who holds the RVM or BEM, should wear the full-size versions of these insignia. The insignia may be worn singly, but if they are mounted with other medals, the entire medal brooch-bar may be worn as it is; there is no need to detach insignia or alter the position of medals on the brooch-bar. In all other circumstances, however, the brooch-bar must not be worn. Insignia or medals are not worn by guests of members (unless they, too, belong to the Order for which a service is being held).

Uniformed Personnel: Personnel who attend these services and wear uniform, should wear the insignia of the Order concerned according to the requirements laid down for the particular uniform being worn. At a service for the Order of the Bath, for example, the holder of a KCB will wear both the Breast Star and the Neck-Badge.

The holder of a Fourth or Fifth Class (Officer/Lieutenant or Member) of an Order, or the Medal of an Order, will wear the entire mounted group of decorations and medals with which it is included. Alternatively, the award may be worn singly.

● **Order of St. John.** Mantles are worn at the Order's services, investitures and on other occasions, such as Priory or Commandery Chapters, by Bailiffs and Dames Grand Cross, Knights and Dames of Justice, and Knights and Dames of Grace. They are also worn by officials of the Order who are Commanders or Officers. The Badge of the Order embellishes the left side of the mantle, and varies in size and material according to the grade of appointment.

Gentlemen: Under the mantle, gentlemen wear a black 'sopra-vest', a vestment of thin black cloth extending from close around the neck to the ankles. The sopra-vest of a Bailiff Grand Cross has on its central breast area a large cloth representation of the Order's Badge. For subsequent grades the sopra-vest is plain, but Knights, Commanders (Brothers) and Chaplains wear their neck-badges from a riband of 38mm (1½ ins.) width so that it hangs about 150mm (6 ins.) below the sopra-vest collar. Medal ribbons are worn in the upper central area of the sopra-vest, and are arranged in accordance with the 'order of wear'.

Ladies: The sopra-vest is not worn by ladies. Under their mantles Dames Grand Cross wear the Sash and Badge of the Order. Dames of Justice, Dames of Grace, Commanders (Sisters), and Officers (Sisters) wear their Badge on a bow on their upper left side under the mantle.

13. Miscellaneous matters

Regulations for the return of insignia on the decease of the holder
There is a requirement that some items of insignia must be returned on the decease of the holder. New recipients are required to sign a covenant undertaking to make arrangements for the return of such insignia after their decease. The following insignia are normally delivered back to the Sovereign by the nearest male relative of the deceased during a private audience, the arrangements for which will have been made after a suitable lapse of time by the Sovereign's Private Secretary:

   (i) The Order of the Garter: the Star, and Sash Badge (the 'Lesser George');
  (ii) The Order of the Thistle: the Star, and Sash Badge;
 (iii) The Order of Merit (awards from 1993)

The following insignia of deceased holders must be returned by their executors direct to the Secretary of the Central Chancery of the Orders of Knighthood, St James's Palace, London SW1A 1BH:

   (i) The Order of the Garter: the garter.
  (ii) The Collars with Badges Appendant of the Orders of the Garter, and of the Thistle; and also of Knight and Dame Grand Cross of the Order of the Bath (GCB).
 (iii) The Collars of Knight and Dame Grand Cross of the Order of St. Michael and St. George (GCMG), the Royal Victorian Order (GCVO), and the Order of the British Empire (GBE).
 (iv) The Royal Victorian Chain.

All other insignia may be retained by the persons legally entitled to receive them under the terms of the will of the deceased.

Loss and replacement of insignia
Recipients are responsible for the safekeeping and insurance of their insignia and medals as they would be for any other valued possessions; this applies especially to insignia which has to be returned at the holder's decease. Insignia which has been damaged or lost through theft, fire or similar circumstances beyond the control of the recipient can usually be replaced, although a charge will be made for the cost of the replacement. In respect of serving personnel replacements may be made at public expense if the loss is due to unavoidable circumstances arising during the course of their duties. In all cases, applications for replacement should be accompanied by a full report of the circumstances of the loss and the action taken to recover the item(s), proof of the loss in the form of a Police report, and/or a claim to an insurance company and a loss assessor's report.

- *Orders of Knighthood and other Insignia.* Applications in respect of the Orders of Knighthood, the Order of Merit, the Order of the Companions of Honour, the Knight Bachelor's Neck-Badge, the Distinguished Service Order, the Imperial Service Order, the Royal Victorian Medal, and the British Empire Medal should be notified to the Central Chancery of the Orders of Knighthood at the earliest opportunity. Insignia which has been lost while in the possession of the 'immediate descendent' of a deceased recipient will be replaced by the Central Chancery on receipt of proof that the descendant is legally entitled to ownership of the insignia, together with proof of the loss. Damage to, or loss of any insignia of the Order of St. John should be notified to the Order's headquarters.

- *Gallantry decorations and gallantry medals.* Applications for the replacement of gallantry awards should, in the case of the George Cross, the George Medal, and the Queen's Gallantry Medal, be submitted directly to the Central Chancery. Those in respect of all other gallantry medals must be made to the Medals Office of the service to which the recipient belongs.

- *Campaign and other medals.*   Applications from serving personnel, in respect of lost or damaged campaign and long service medals are handled by the Medal Offices of the respective services. The Ministry of Defence does not consider applications for loss from ex-servicemen unless the loss has been sustained through theft or accidental destruction. Applications in respect of coronation and jubilee medals should be referred to the Central Chancery of the Orders of Knighthood.

- *Warrants of Appointment.* Certified copies of lost Warrants of Appointment can be obtained on application from the Central Chancery.

- *Foreign orders, decorations and medals.* Enquiries in connection with the loss and replacement of foreign awards should in the first instance be made to the embassy or high commission of the country concerned.

Wearing of medals by next-of-kin

In the United Kingdom the practice has developed of next-of-kin or near relatives wearing the medals of deceased servicemen at services of Remembrance and similar public occasions on the *right* side of civilian attire. It must be emphasised, however, that this practice carries absolutely no official sanction, and any person in authority will maintain this line when asked for advice.

Unofficial Commemorative Medals

Various unofficial commemorative medals have been produced and sold in recent years by medal dealers and manufacturers. A Defence Council Instruction issued by the Ministry of Defence in 2000 reminds Crown servants that these - as well as other categories of unauthorised decorations - must not be worn with uniform. Although this stricture does not, technically speaking, apply to ex-servicemen, it should be borne in mind that while the selling of unofficial commemorative medals often involves the laudable purpose of raising money for veterans' charities and associations, the medals themselves do not have the status of official medals that have been authorised by the Sovereign, and should not therefore be publicly worn with those issued officially. The practice, which is sometimes advocated, of wearing commemorative medals mounted on a separate brooch-bar beneath any official medals is not authorised as only one medal brooch-bar may be worn on the left side with civilian dress, and only certain specified medals are approved for wear on the right side.

14.   Glossary of terms

Beckets   Beckets are the means by which medal brooch-bars or the stars of Orders of Knighthood are attached in their correct positions on uniforms or coats.   They are small material loops or eyelets, of the same cloth and colour as the garment, which are sewn in to position, thus enabling the pin of a star or brooch-bar to pass through and be secured.   Beckets need to be accurately situated and sewn and require the attention of a capable tailor.

Bars and Clasps   A 'bar' is not, as is so often assumed, the same thing as a 'clasp'. A bar to a decoration or medal (usually denoting a second award of the same medal) is a full-width metal strip affixed to the riband; a clasp (usually citing the campaign area in which the wearer has served) is a similar full-width strip but is attached or 'clasped' by means of rivets or pins to the medal's riband suspension pin.   Each successive clasp is fitted to the one beneath it.

Badges   The term 'badge' usually refers to the main distinguishing component, or symbol, of an Order of Knighthood or a decoration.   The badge of an Order having three or five classes features in each class, a sash badge, neck-badge and breast badge being differentiated from each other by size and/or variations in design.   Some confusion can arise over the term 'breast badge'; in one or two cases (such as the Knight Bachelor's Badge) it can describe a piece of insignia which though unlike the star of an Order, is nevertheless attached to the coat in the same fashion.   Otherwise, a 'breast badge' describes the Fourth or Fifth Class insignia of an Order which is suspended from a short riband and worn in the same fashion as a medal.

Decoration   This term has both specific and general areas of usage.   Its main application within the context of this work is to identify the series of senior awards for gallantry and distinguished conduct.   Unlike 'medals', decorations are usually in the style of enamel or metal crosses, but are nevertheless suspended from short ribands and worn in the same manner as medals.   A 'decoration' may nevertheless refer to a gallantry award which is in the form of a medal.   The term can also be used when referring to a neck-badge (i.e. 'neck decoration'), or a ladies' badge suspended from a bow (i.e 'ladies' bow decoration'), or to the Fourth or Fifth Class breast badge of an Order of Knighthood.   It can in addition refer to orders, decorations and medals in the general sense, as when, for example, it is used on invitations to indicate a requirement that insignia should be worn.

Insignia   By this term is meant all or any such items as stars, collars, neck-badges, ribands, medals, decorations, and so on.

Medal   In the United Kingdom the term 'medal' covers the broad range of awards which are usually of a standard circular form, silver (but sometimes of gold or bronze), and worn suspended from a short riband.

Miniatures   These are miniature copies of the badges of the Orders of Knighthood, and of decorations and medals. They are mounted on a miniature medal brooch-bar and worn with Mess Dress or civilian Evening Dress.

Order of Wear   This is the correct sequence, officially laid down by the Lord Chamberlain's Office, in which orders, decorations and medals should be worn. It is sometimes confused with the 'order of precedence' which governs the order in which people are placed, rather than insignia. It is quite proper, however, to speak of one decoration or medal as having 'precedence' over another.

Riband/Ribbon   The term 'riband' refers to the material from which any item of insignia is suspended. It should not, however, be confused with the term 'ribbon' which refers to the riband material of an order, decoration or medal when worn alone, being either sewn directly on to a uniform coat or mounted for this purpose on a brooch.

Table 1: Summary of insignia requirements and restrictions for Civilian Dress

	INSIGNIA	EVENING DRESS 'WHITE TIE'		EVENING DRESS 'BLACK TIE'	
		Gentlemen Full Evening Dress	Ladies Long Dress	Gentlemen Dinner Jacket	Ladies Long/Short Dress
Evening	Broad Riband	Yes	Yes	Not worn	Not worn
	Breast Star maximum	4	4	1	1
	Neck Badge/Bow	1	1	1	1
	Decorations and Medals (Miniatures)	Yes	Yes	Yes	Yes
Day		DAY DRESS I		DAY DRESS II	
		Gentlemen Morning Dress	Ladies Formal Day Dress	Gentlemen Lounge Suit	Ladies Day Dress
	Collar	Only when specially ordered	Only when specially ordered	Not worn	Not worn
	Broad Riband	Not worn	Not worn	Not worn	Not worn
	Breast Stars	1 (but exceptionally up to 4)	1 (but exceptionally up to 4)	Not worn	Not worn
	Neck-Badge/Bow	1	1	1	1
	Decorations and Medals (Full-size)	Yes	Yes	Yes	Yes

Notes to Table 2 (p. 111):

[1] Maximum of four breast stars with the RM Full Ceremonial Dress, two with No. 1A Blue Dress.

[2] Maximum of three breast stars with RAF No. 1A Dress, but may increase to four if the star of a foreign order is worn.

[3] Maximum of three neck decorations with RN Ceremonial Day Coat (but two for Joint Service events), and two with No. 1A Dress.

[4] Maximum of three neck decorations with RM Full Ceremonial Dress (but two for Joint Service events), and two with No. 1A Blue Dress.

[5] One neck decoration only with General Officer's Frock Coat (but two for Joint Service events).

[6] Maximum of three neck decorations with Full Dress and No 1 Dress (Ceremonial), but maximum of two for Joint Service events.

Table 2: Summary of insignia requirements and restrictions for the Armed Forces

	INSIGNIA	RN	RM	ARMY			RAF
Full ceremonial day		Ceremonial Day/No. 1A Dress	Full Cereml./No 1A Blue Dress	Frock Coat	Full Dress/No 1 Dress with accoutrements	No 1 Dress with Sam Browne belt	No 1A Dress (ceremonial), No 1 Dress
	Collar/Broad Riband	Yes	Full Cereml. only	Yes	Yes	No	Yes
	Stars maximum	4	4(2)[1]	4	4	2	3(4)[2]
	Neck Decorations	3(2)[3]	3(2)[4]	1(2)[5]	3(2)[6]	2	2
	Medals	Yes	Yes	Yes	Yes	Yes	Yes
Ceremonial day		No 1B Dress Blue Dress	No 1A Blue Dress or 1B Lovat Dress	Frock Coat	No 1 Dress with accoutrements Sam Browne belt	No 1 Dress or No 2 Dress with No 1 Dress	No 1A Dress (ceremonial),
	Collar/Broad Riband	Not worn	Not worn	Not worn	Not worn	Not worn	Not worn
	Stars maximum	2	2	2	2	2	2
	Neck Decorations	1	1	1	1	1	1
	Medals	Yes	Yes	Yes	Yes	Yes	Yes
Non-ceremonial day		No 1C Dress Undress	No 1A Blue Dress or 1C Lovat Dress	Frock Coat	No 1 Dress	No 2 Dress	No 1 Dress
	Collar/Broad Riband	Not worn	Not worn	Not worn	Not worn	Not worn	Not worn
	Stars maximum	None worn	None worn	None worn	None worn	None worn	None worn
	Neck Decorations	None worn	None worn	None worn	None worn	None worn	None worn
	Medal Ribbons	Yes	Yes	Yes	Yes	Yes	Yes
Full ceremonial evening		No 2A Formal Evening Dress	No. 2A Formal Evening Dress		No 10 Mess Dress		No 5A Mess Dress White Waistcoat
	Broad Riband	Yes	Yes		Yes		Yes
	Stars maximum	4	4		4		4
	Neck Decorations	1	1		1		1
	Miniature Medals	Yes	Yes		Yes		Yes
Ceremonial evening		No 2B Formal Evening Dress	No. 2B Formal Evening Dress		No 10 Mess Dress		No 5B Mess Dress Blue Waistcoat
	Broad Riband	Not worn	Not worn		Not worn		Not worn
	Stars maximum	2	2		2		2
	Neck Decorations	1	1		1		1
	Miniature Medals	Yes	Yes		Yes		Yes
Non-ceremonial evening		No 2B Evening Dress	No. 2B Evening Dress		No 10 Mess Dress		No 5B Mess Dress Waistcoat/C'bund
	Miniature Medals	Yes	Yes		Yes		Yes
	Miniature Medal Ribbons	Not worn	Not worn		Not worn		Not worn

Appendix 1 ~ British Campaign Medals and Clasps

This Appendix provides details of the clasps available for each of the campaign medals listed in Section 5, 'Order of Wear'. The dates in italic indicate the date of campaign if this does not appear on the clasp itself. The earliest clasps awarded for the older General Service Medals are not shown, and the medals themselves have therefore been placed according to the date of the earliest clasps here noted.

Campaign Medals	Clasps
1914 Star	5 Aug : 22 Nov 1914
1914-15 Star	*none*
British War Medal	*none*
Mercantile Marine Medal	*none*
Victory Medal	*none*
Territorial Force War Medal	*none*
General Service Medal (Army and RAF) 1918-62	S. Persia *1918-19*
	Kurdistan *1919-23*
	Iraq *1919-20*
	NW Persia *1920*
	Southern Desert: Iraq *1928*
	Northern Kurdistan *1932*
	Palestine *1936-39*
	Bomb & Mine Clearance 1945-49
	Bomb & Mine Clearance 1945-56
	South East Asia 1945-46
	Palestine 1945-48
	Malaya *1948-60*
	Canal Zone *1951-54*
	Cyprus *1955-59*
	Near East *1956*
	Arabian Peninsula *1957-60*
	Brunei *1962*
India General Service Medal 1908-35	Afghanistan NWF 1919
	Waziristan 1919-21
	Mahsud 1919-20
	Malabar 1921-22
	Waziristan 1921-24
	Waziristan 1925
	North West Frontier 1930-31
	Burma 1930-32

	Mohmand 1933
	North West Frontier 1935
Naval General Service Medal 1915-62	Iraq 1919-20
	NW Persia 1920
	Palestine 1936-39
	SE Asia 1945-46
	Minesweeping 1945-51
	Palestine 1945-48
	Malaya *1948-60*
	Yangtze 1949
	Bomb & Mine Clearance 1945-53
	Bomb & Mine Clearance 1945-46
	Canal Zone *1951-54*
	Bomb & Mine Clearance Mediterranean *1955-60*
	Cyprus *1955-59*
	Near East *1956*
	Arabian Peninsula *1957-60*
	Brunei *1962*
India General Service Medal 1936-9	North West Frontier 1936-37
	North West Frontier 1937-39
1939-45 Star	Battle of Britain *1940*
Atlantic Star	Air Crew Europe *1939-44*
	France and Germany *1944-45*
Air Crew Europe Star	Atlantic *1939-45*
	France and Germany *1944-45*
Africa Star	North Africa 1942-43
	8th Army *1942-43*
	1st Army *1942-43*
Pacific Star	Burma *1941-45*
Burma Star	Pacific *1941-45*
Italy Star	*none*
France and Germany Star	Atlantic *1944-45*
Defence Medal	*none*
Canadian Volunteer Service Medal	*maple leaf bar*
	Dieppe *19 Aug. 1942*
	Hong Kong *8-25 Dec. 1941*
1939-45 War Medal	*none*
1939-45 Africa Service Medal of the Union of South Africa	*none*
India Service Medal	*none*
New Zealand War Service Medal	*none*
Southern Rhodesia Service Medal	*none*
Australian Service Medal	*none*

Korea Medal *1950-53*   *none*
Africa General Service Medal   Kenya *1952-56*
General Service Medal 1962-   Borneo *1962-66*
                                            South Vietnam *1962-64*
                                            Radfan *1964*
                                            South Arabia *1964-67*
                                            Malay Peninsula *1964-66*
                                            Northern Ireland *1969-*
                                            Dhofar *1969-76*
                                            Lebanon *1983-84*
                                            Mine Clearance-Gulf of Suez *1984*
                                            Gulf *1986-89*
                                            Kuwait *1991*
                                            N. Iraq & S. Turkey *1991*
                                            Air Operations Iraq *1991-2003*
Vietnam Medal *1964-73**   *none*
South Atlantic Medal *1982*   *rosette*
Gulf Medal *1990-1*   2 Aug 1990
                                            16 Jan - 28 Feb 1991

Operational Service Medal *2000-*
    Sierra Leone 1999-2002   *rosette* (for Operations Maidenly and Barras)
    Afghanistan 2001-   Afghanistan
Iraq Medal *2003*   19 Mar – 28 Apr 2003

* The Vietnam Medal was instituted by the Sovereign and awarded chiefly to Australian and New Zealand forces. When worn by British servicemen it is worn as a Commonwealth award after British medals.

Appendix 2 ~ United Nations, NATO and other international medals

This Appendix serves as an annex to Section 5, 'Order of Wear' and lists the medals awarded by international institutions for which British forces have qualified.

United Nations Medals:
UN Korea Service Medal (1950-54)
ONUC: Organisation des Nations Unies au Congo (1960-64)
UNFICYP: United Nations Force in Cyprus (1964-)
UNIFIL: United Nations Interim Force in Lebanon (1978-)
UNTAG: United Nations Transitional Assistance Group (Namibia 1989-90)
UNIKOM: United Nations Iraq Kuwait Observation Mission (1991-)
MINURSO: Mission des Nations Unies pour la Referendum dans le Sahara Occidental (1991-)
UNAMIC: United Nations Advanced Mission in Cambodia (1991-92)
UNTAC: United Nations Transitional Authority in Cambodia (1992-93)
UNPROFOR: United Nations Protection Force, Bosnia-Herzegovina (1992-95)
UNPROFOR with UNCRO clasp (Confidence Restoration Operation in Croatia, 1995-96)
UNOSOM: United Nations Operations in Somalia (1992-95)
ONUMOZ: Operations des Nations Unies pour le referendum dans Mozambique (1992-95)
UNOMIG: United Nations Observer Mission in Georgia (1993-96)
UNAMIR: United Nations Assistance Mission in Rwanda (1993-96)
UNOMIL: United Nations Observer Mission in Liberia (1993-97)
UNMIBH: United Nations Mission in Bosnia Herzegovena (1995-)
UNAVEM III: United Nations Angola Verification Mission (1995-97)
UNPREDEP: United Nations Preventative Deployment in the former Republic of Macedonia (1995-99)
UNTAES: United Nations Transitional Authority in Eastern Slavonia, Baranja and Western Sirmium (1995-98)
UNMOP: United Nations Mission of Observers in Prevlaka (1996-)
UNOMSIL: United Nations Observer Mission in Sierra Leone (1998-99)
UNAMSIL: United Nations Mission in Sierra Leone (1999-)
UNAMET/UNTAET: United Nations Mission in East Timor /United Nations Transitional Administration in East Timor (1999-)
UNMIK: United Nations Interim Administration in Kosovo (1999-)
MONUC: United Nations Mission in the Congo (2000-)
UNMEE: United Nations Mission in Ethiopia and Eritrea (2000-)

United Nations Special Service Medal, with the following bars:
(UNOCHA) Afghanistan (1989-90)
Former Yugoslavia (July 1992-Jan. 1996)

NATO Medals:
The NATO Medal, former Yugoslavia 1994
The NATO Medal, Kosovo 2000
The NATO Medal, Macedonia 2002
The NATO Medal, Article 5 Eagle Assist Operation 2003*
The NATO Medal, Article 5 Active Endeavour Operation 2003*
The NATO Medal, Balkans 2003
The NATO Meritorious Service Medal*

Other international medals:
Multinational Force and Observers Medal (Sinai Peninsula, 1982)
The European Community Military Mission in Yugoslavia Medal, 1991
The Western European Union Mission Service Medal, 1994

* These medals have not been approved for wear although they may have been received.

Appendix 3 ~ Riband widths with insignia and on ribbon bars

The widths of ribands given here are those specified when ribands are required to be worn in their full-width state. It should be noted, however, that in most cases regulations require neck decorations to be suspended from ribands of miniature width of 16mm (⅝ in.) when worn by men in civilian dress and most types of uniform, and by women in uniform. *The insignia listed below is not in strict order of precedence.*

	With Insignia	Ribbon Bars
KG and LG	102mm (4 ins.)	Not worn
KT and LT	102mm (4 ins.)	Not worn
GCB	102mm (4 ins.)	38mm (1½ ins.)
Dames Grand Cross (GCB)	57mm (2¼ ins.)	38mm (1½ ins.)
KCB	51mm (2 ins.)	38mm (1½ ins.)
DCB	45mm (1¾ ins)	38mm (1½ ins.)
CB	38mm (1½ ins.)	38mm (1½ ins.)
Order of Merit	51mm (2 ins.)	51mm (2 ins.)
GCMG	102mm (4 ins.)	38mm (1½ ins.)
Dames Grand Cross (GCMG)	57mm (2 ¼ ins.)	38mm (1½ ins.)
KCMG	51mm (2 ins.)	38mm (1½ ins.)
DCMG	45mm (1¾ ins.)	38mm (1½ ins.)
CMG	38mm (1½ ins.)	38mm (1½ ins.)
GCVO	95mm (3¾ ins.)	32mm (1¼ ins.)
Dames Grand Cross (GCVO)	57mm (2¼ ins.)	32mm (1¼ ins.)
KCVO	45mm (1¾ ins.)	32mm (1¼ ins.)
DCVO	45mm (1¾ ins.)	32mm (1¼ ins.)
CVO	45mm (1¾ ins.)	32mm (1¼ ins.)
LVO	32mm (1¼ ins.)	32mm (1¼ ins.)
MVO	32mm (1¼ ins.)	32mm (1¼ ins.)
RVM	32mm (1¼ ins.)	32mm (1¼ ins.)
GBE	102mm (4 ins.)	38mm (1½ ins.)
Dames Grand Cross (GBE)	57mm (2¼ ins.)	38mm (1½ ins.)
KBE	45mm (1¾ ins.)	38mm (1½ ins.)
DBE	45mm (1¾ ins.)	38mm (1½ ins.)
CBE	45mm (1¾ ins.)	38mm (1½ ins.)
OBE	38mm (1½ ins.)	38mm (1½ ins.)
MBE	38mm (1½ ins.)	38mm (1½ ins.)
BEM	32mm (1¼ ins.)	32mm (1¼ ins.)
Companion of Honour	38mm (1½ ins.)	38mm (1½ ins.)
Distinguished Service Order	29mm (1⅛ ins.)	29mm (1⅛ ins.)

	With Insignia	**Ribbon Bars**
Baronet's Badge	45mm (1¾ ins.)	Not worn
Knight Bachelor's Badge	38mm (1½ ins.)	38mm (1½ ins.)

Order of St. John:

	With Insignia	**Ribbon Bars**
Bailiffs Grand Cross	102mm (4 ins.)	38mm (1½ ins.)
Dames Grand Cross	57mm (2¼ ins.)	38mm (1½ ins.)
Knights of Justice		
Dames of Justice		
Knights of Grace		
Dames of Grace		
Chaplain		
Commander (Brother)	38mm (1½ ins.)	38mm (1½ ins.)
Commander (Sister)		
Officer (Brother)		
Officer (Sister)		
Serving Brother		
Serving Sister		

Appendix 4 ~ Permitted post-nominal letters of British Orders, Decorations and Medals

Post-nominal letters denoting membership of an Order of Knighthood or the award of a decoration for gallantry or meritorious service may only be used where expressly permitted under the Statutes of an order or decoration. Holders of the awards listed below may use the appropriate post-nominal letters according to the sequence set out in the 'Order of Wear' (Section 5); there is no official limit to the number of sets of post-nominal letters that may be used after a name.

Post-nominal letters should be grouped after a person's name in the following sequence: (1) Bt (Baronet), Esq (Esquire); (2) Orders, Decorations and Medals; (3) Appointments (eg. PC, ADC, QC, DL, JP, MP); (4) University degrees and honorary degrees (in order of the date of award); (5) Religious Orders and medical qualifications; (6) Fellowships of learned societies; Fellowships, Membership of Professional Institutions, Associations; (7) Membership of the Armed Forces (eg. RN, RNR, RM, RE, RAMC, RAF).

Post-nominal letters are not used to denote 'Knight Bachelor', and may not be used to denote honorary awards of Commonwealth or foreign orders and decorations.

Royal Victorian Order and *Order of the British Empire*. Members of these Orders who are also holders of the Medal of their Order may in addition use the postnominal letters of 'RVM' and 'BEM'. Persons who hold two appointments in the Order of the British Empire use the postnominal letters for the *senior* Class awarded.

Order of St. John of Jerusalem. Post-nominals are used by members of the Order only in connection with official business relating to the Order.

Air Efficiency Award	AE[1]
Air Force Cross	AFC
Air Force Medal	AFM
Albert Medal	AM
Associate, Royal Red Cross (2nd Class)	ARRC
Baronet	Bt[2]
British Empire Medal	BEM

---

[1] Air Efficiency Award – the right to use letters applies only when awarded to officers.
[2] Baronet's Badge – the letters 'Bt' (or 'Bart' in more antiquated usage) are shown immediately after the surname and before all other post nominal letters.

Canadian Forces Decoration	CD
Colonial Police Medal (for Gallantry)	CPM
Colonial Police Medal for Meritorious Service	CPMSM
Commander, Order of the British Empire	CBE
Commander, Royal Victorian Order	CVO
Companions of Honour, Member of the Order of	CH
Companion, Order of the Bath	CB
Companion, Order of St. Michael and St. George	CMG
Companion, Order of the Indian Empire	CIE
Companion, Order of the Star of India	CSI
Conspicuous Gallantry Cross	CGC
Conspicuous Gallantry Medal	CGM
Crown of India, Lady of the Imperial Order of the	CI
Dame Commander, Order of the Bath	DCB
Dame Commander, Order of St. Michael and St. George	DCMG
Dame Commander, Royal Victorian Order	DCVO
Dame Commander, Order of the British Empire	DBE
Distinguished Conduct Medal	DCM
Distinguished Flying Cross	DFC
Distinguished Flying Medal	DFM
Distinguished Service Cross	DSC
Distinguished Service Medal	DSM
Distinguished Service Order	DSO
Efficiency Decoration	ED
George Cross	GC
George Medal	GM
Imperial Service Order	ISO
Indian Distinguished Service Medal	IDSM
Indian Order of Merit	IOM
King's Fire Service Medal (for Gallantry)	KFSM
King's Police Medal (for Gallantry)	KPM
Knight Companion, Order of the Garter	KG
Knight, Order of the Thistle	KT
Knight, Order of St Patrick	KP
Knight / Dame Grand Cross, Order of the Bath	GCB
Knight / Dame Grand Cross, Order of St. Michael and St. George	GCMG
Knight / Dame Grand Cross, Royal Victorian Order	GCVO
Knight / Dame Grand Cross, Order of the British Empire	GBE
Knight Commander, Order of the Bath	KCB
Knight Commander, Order of St. Michael and St. George	KCMG

Knight Commander, Royal Victorian Order	KCVO
Knight Commander, Order of the British Empire	KBE
Lady Companion, Order of the Garter	LG
Lady, Order of the Thistle	LT
Lieutenant, Royal Victorian Order	LVO
Member, Order of the British Empire	MBE
Member, Royal Victorian Order	MVO
Meritorious Service Medal	MSM[3]
Military Cross	MC
Military Medal	MM
Officer, Order of the British Empire	OBE
Order of British India	OBI
Order of Merit, Member	OM
Queen's Fire Service Medal for Distinguished Service	QFSM
Queen's Gallantry Medal	QGM
Queen's Police Medal	QPM
Queen's Volunteer Reserves Medal	QVRM
Royal Naval Reserve Decoration	RD
Royal Naval Volunteer Reserve Officers' Decoration	VRD
Royal Red Cross (1st Class)	RRC
Royal Victorian Medal	RVM
Sea Gallantry Medal	SGM
Territorial Decoration	TD
Ulster Defence Regiment Medal	UD[4]
Victoria Cross	VC

[3] Meritorious Service Medal – the right to use these letters only applies if it was awarded in the Royal Navy before 20 July 1928.
[4] Ulster Defence Regiment Medal – the right to use letters applies only when awarded to officers.

Appendix 5 ~ Addresses

The Secretary,
The Central Chancery of the Orders of Knighthood,
St. James's Palace,
London SW1A 1BG.
  tel: 0207 930 4832

Imperial Society of Knights Bachelor,
21, Old Building,
Lincoln's Inn,
London WC2A 3UJ.
  tel: 0207 405 1860

The Most Venerable Order of the Hospital of St. John of Jerusalem,
Priory House,
25, St. John's Lane,
Clerkenwell,
London EC1M 4PP.
  tel: 0207 251 3292
  www.orderofstjohn.org

The Ceremonial Secretariat (Honours),
Cabinet Office,
35, Great Smith Street,
London SW1P 3BQ.
  www.cabinet-office.gov.uk/ceremonial

Claims for campaign medals, Royal Navy:
Royal Naval Medal Office,
Room 1068,
Centurion Building,
Grange Road,
Gosport,
Hampshire PO13 9XA.

Claims for campaign medals, Royal Marines:
Royal Marines Medal Office,
Room 038,
Centurion Building,
Grange Road,
Gosport,
Hampshire PO13 9XA.

Claims for campaign medals, Army:
Army Medal Office,
Building 250,
RAF Innesworth,
Gloucester,
Gloucestershire GL3 1HW.

Claims for campaign medals, RAF:
Royal Air Force Medal Office,
Room 6,
PMA(Sec)1c (RAF),
Building 248A,
RAF Innesworth,
Gloucester,
Gloucestershire GL3 1EZ.

Claims for campaign medals, RFA:
Royal Fleet Auxiliary Medal Office,
SOS RFA CS1A,
Room F11,
Lancelot Building,
PP29,
HM Naval Base,
Portsmouth,
Hampshire PO1 3NH.

The Officer-in-Waiting,
College of Arms,
Queen Victoria Street,
London EC4V 4BT.
 tel: 0207 248 2762
 www.college-of-arms.gov.uk

The Court of the Lord Lyon,
HM New Register House,
Edinburgh EH1 3YT.
 tel: 0131 556 7255
 www.lyon-court.com

The Secretary,
VC and GC Association,
Horse Guards,
Whitehall,
London SW1A 2AX.
 tel: 0207 930 3506

Index

academic robes 102
Armed Forces,
   awards prior to enlistment 73
   foreign awards 72-73
   services for Orders of Knighthood 103-104
armorial bearings 7-8
Army,
   ceremonial and other uniforms 88-89
   medal ribbons 88
   uniforms:
      Full Dress 82-83
      No. 1 Dress (Ceremonial) 82-83
      No. 3 Dress (Ceremonial, Warm
        Weather) 82-83
      Frock Coat 83-84
      No. 1 (and No. 3) Dress 85-87
      No. 2 (Service Dress) and No. 4
        (Warm Weather Service Dress) 85-87
      No. 6 Dress 87
      Mess Dress 94-97

Baronets' Badge 4
bars 39-40
Bath, Order of the,
   insignia and classes 1-2
beckets 31, 38
bow decorations, ladies' 33-34
   full evening dress 63-64
   evening dress ('black tie') 66-67
   formal day dress 70
   day dress 70-71
bow decoration,
   sash badge worn as 67
British Empire, Order of the,
   British Empire Medal 10
   'double awards' in 10-11
   Gallantry awards 11
   insignia and classes 3

order of wear, Civil and Military
   divisions 38-39
ribbons, arrangement of (double
   (awards) 45-46

campaign medals,
   arrangement of 39
   emblems 40-41
   list of clasps 112-114
ceremonial uniforms 100-101
clasps 39-40
clergymen and clerical robes 102
collars and badges of Orders of
   Knighthood 30
   gentlemen, morning dress 57
   ladies, formal day dress 68-69
   with peers' and peeresses' robes 98-99
   worn at services for Orders of
      Knighthood 103
   Armed Forces uniform 73-74
Commonwealth awards 13-14
Companions of Honour, Order of the 3
court dress 100

daytime functions,
   orders, decorations and medals
      worn at 17-18

emblems,
   Order of the British Empire,
      Gallantry 40
   campaign medals 40
   international medals (UN, NATO) 41
evening functions
   orders, decorations and medals
   worn at 18-20

foreign awards 12-16
   arrangement on medal-bar 14-15, 43-44

protocol for wearing 14-16
restricted permission to wear 13
ribbon rosettes 48
unrestricted permission to wear 12-13

Garter, Order of the
insignia 1
gentlemen,
full evening dress 51-55
dinner jacket 55-57
morning dress 57-59
lounge suit 59-61

honorary awards to non-British
subjects 7
honours, announcements of 6
honours lists 6

insignia,
loss and replacement of 105-106
return to Central Chancery upon
death of holder 105
investitures
award presented abroad 8
awards qualifying for presentation
at investiture 8
dress requirements at 9
Order of St. John 9
posthumous awards 9

judges' robes 99

Knight Bachelor,
insignia 4, 32-33
promotion to Order of
Knighthood 11
knighthood, accolade of 9-10

ladies,
full evening dress 62-65
evening dress ('black tie') 65-67
formal day dress (morning dress) 67-70
day dress 70-71
London Gazette, The 6, 12

medals,
arrangement on medal-bar 38-39
presentation of 8-9
court style mounting 37-38
ordinary style mounting 35-37
international (UN, NATO, etc) 39
list of 115-116
worn on right side 39
worn by ladies 44-45, 67-71
medal-bar, method of attachment 38-39
Mention in Despatches emblem 41-42, 47-48
Merit, Order of 3
correct method of display 32
mess dress (Royal Navy, Royal Marines,
Army, and Royal Air Force) 94-97
miniatures 48-50
arrangement by precedence 49
emblems 50
entitlement to wear from award
date 7
ladies' 50
Orders of Knighthood 48-49
when not worn 49
municipal robes 101

neck decorations 31-32
gentlemen, full evening dress 53
dinner jacket 55
morning dress 59
lounge suit 59-60
sash badge worn as 55-56
next-of-kin,
wearing of medals by 106

Orders of Knighthood,
badges 38
insignia and classes 1-3
promotion in 9-10
services of dedication, insignia
worn at 103-104
order of wear 21-29

peers' and peeresses' robes 98-99

police uniform   101
post-nominal letters,
   use of   6-7
   list of those permitted   119-121
precedence, *see* order of wear

Queen's Commendation emblems
         42-43, 47-48
Queen's Counsels' robes   99
riband widths   117-118
ribbons and ribbon bars   45-46
ribbons,
   commencement of wear   7, 46
   emblems   46-48
Royal Air Force,
   medal ribbons   93
   uniforms:
      No. 1 Dress   90-92
      No. 1A Dress   90-92
      No. 6 Dress   90-92
      Mess Dress   94-97
Royal Marines,
   medal ribbons   81
   uniforms:
      Full Ceremonial Dress   80
      No. 1A Blue Dress   80-81
      No. 1B Lovat Dress   80-81
      Mess Dress   94-97
Royal Navy,
   medal ribbons   79-80
   ratings' medals   79
   uniforms:
      Ceremonial Day Coat   75-78
      No. 1A (and 1AW) Dress   75-78
      No. 1B (and 1BW) Dress   78
      No. 1C (and 1CW) Dress   79-80
      Mess Dress   94-97
Royal Victorian Chain   4
   treated as neck decoration   32
Royal Victorian Order,
   'double awards' in   10
   insignia and classes   2-3

St. John, Order of,
   insignia and grades   5
   investitures   9
   services and robes   104
St. Michael & St. George, Order of,
   correct method of displaying
      badge   32
   insignia and classes   2
sashes and badges   30-31
   worn with Armed Forces uniforms
         73-74
      Mess Dress   94
   ceremonial uniform   100-101
   gentlemen, full evening dress   51
   ladies, full evening dress   62
sash badges,
   worn as neck decorations (men)
         31, 55-56
   worn as bow decorations (ladies) 31, 67
stars, breast   31
   gentlemen, full evening dress   51-52
      dinner jacket   55
      morning dress   57-58
   ladies, full evening dress   62
      evening dress ('black tie')   66
      formal day dress   69
   method of attachment   31
   Armed Forces uniform (and
      see individual service uniforms)
         74-93

Thistle, Order of the,
   insignia   1
titles of 'Sir' and 'Dame',
   use of, from gazetting of award   6-7

uniforms, *see* under Army, Royal Navy,
   Royal Marines, Royal Air Force,
   ceremonial uniforms
unofficial medals   106-107